W9-CBR-990

David Lynch

THE MAN FROM ANOTHER PLACE

DENNIS LIM

ICONS SERIES

New Harvest
Houghton Mifflin Harcourt
BOSTON • NEW YORK
2015

This edition published by special arrangement with Amazon Publishing

For information about permission to reproduce selections from this book, go to www.apub.com.

www.hmhco.com

Library of Congress Cataloging-in-Publication Data
Lim, Dennis, date.
David Lynch : the man from another place / Dennis Lim.
pages cm. — (Icons series)
ISBN 978-0-544-34375-7 (hardback)
1. Lynch, David, date. — Criticism and interpretation. I. Title.
PN1998.3.L96L56 2015
791.4302'33092 — dc23
2015015903

Printed in the United States of America
DOC 10 9 8 7 6 5 4 3 2 1

For John

Contents

Weird on Top

THERE ARE FOUR turning points in the creative life of David Lynch, four decisive moments that turned a common Irish last name into an adjective for our time.

1961: In Alexandria, Virginia, a girlfriend introduces fifteen-year-old David Lynch to a boy named Toby Keeler, whose father, Bushnell, is an artist. The senior Keeler paints landscapes, still lifes, nautical scenes: mantelpiece art, good enough to sell. Lynch, visiting his studio, is shocked to learn it's possible to make a living that way. Bushnell Keeler gives the boy a book called *The Art Spirit* by the painter Robert Henri. A leader of the realist movement known as the Ashcan school, which favored gritty urban scenes and rallied around the credo "art for life's sake," Henri was also an inspirational teacher (of Edward Hopper and George Bellows, among others). The book is a collection of his notes and talks to students, combining technical instruction with musings on art as the source of "our greatest happiness," peppered with motivational refrains ("Do some great work, Son!"). For the teenage Lynch, it changes everything, becomes a symbol of possibility. He decides to dedicate himself to the noble and romantic pursuit of art making, or, as he likes to call it, the "art life."

1967: Lynch is now a painting student at the Pennsylvania Academy of the Fine Arts, where, as it happens, Robert Henri studied in the 1880s. Lynch has landed in Philadelphia after a brief stint at the School of the Museum of Fine Arts in Boston and an abortive trip to Europe to study with the expressionist painter Oskar Kokoschka. For a small-town boy, the violence and squalor of Philly—especially in Lynch's run-down post-industrial neighborhood—is nightmarish but it's also where he starts to find his footing as an artist, where he has his "first original thought." His paintings become literally and figuratively darker. One afternoon, while he's working on a nearly all-black painting of a garden at night, he senses a wind emanating from within the canvas, seeming to stir the leaves under his brush. He wonders: What if paintings could move? What if they had sound? For the school's annual contest a few months later, Lynch submits a mixed-media piece: a sculpted screen onto which he projects a stop-motion animated loop that depicts, over and over, a row of figures in agony, their stomachs and esophageal tracts filling up with red liquid that is expelled in a collective retch, accompanied by the sound of a blaring siren. He calls this, his first film, *Six Men Getting Sick*. It shares the first prize.

1973: As much as Lynch loves his new home of Los Angeles—where he relocated with his artist wife, Peggy, and their baby daughter, Jennifer, to enroll at the brand-new American Film Institute Conservatory in 1969—this is a low moment for him. He's mired in the seemingly interminable production of his first feature, *Eraserhead;* the stop-start no-budget shoot will drag on for three more years. The responsibilities of being a family man in his midtwenties are also taking a toll. Anxious and depressed, he loses his temper frequently. His sister, Martha, recommends Transcendental Meditation, which she started practicing a few months earlier. TM is a technique pioneered by the Maharishi Mahesh Yogi, known as a spiritual guru to the stars, including the Beatles. Skeptical but curious, Lynch visits the TM center in Los Angeles, where an instructor—she resembles

Doris Day, he will later recall — assigns him a mantra, a "sound-vibration-thought" that he is to focus on for twenty minutes with his eyes closed. The experience is so overwhelming — "pure bliss" — that he doesn't notice time elapsing. A creature of habit, Lynch claims to have never missed a session since: twenty minutes, twice a day. He credits TM with increasing his "flow of creativity" and always has a notepad and pen by his side when he meditates.

The fourth moment is harder to locate. Perhaps it is after his most notorious flop, *Dune,* which prompts him to declare that he would rather not make a film than make one that would not allow him final cut. Perhaps it is after the cancellation of his most surprising success, the TV series *Twin Peaks,* which causes him to write, in capital letters, on a wooden board, I WILL NEVER WORK IN TELEVISION AGAIN. (He will break the promise, more than once.) Perhaps it comes earlier, in the transition from painting, a solo activity, to cinema, a collaborative endeavor, but one that he approaches in the identical spirit of absolute control. Or even before that, during a nomadic childhood that he associates most indelibly with Montana, with its Wild West history and individualist mythology. Whenever it may be, Lynch acquires the will or temperament it takes to be an artist who is never less than fully himself, even within an industrial medium and against the flattening forces of the mainstream.

More than five years after the start of shooting, *Eraserhead* premiered at the Filmex festival in Los Angeles in March 1977. It was reviewed in *Variety* under the headline "Dismal American Film Institute Exercise in Gore; Commercial Prospects Nil." As a midnight movie, it ran for more than three years in New York City and Los Angeles, grossing $7 million in the United States alone, seventy times its shoestring budget. His follow-up, *The Elephant Man,* produced by Mel Brooks, earned him

an Academy Award nomination. His next film, *Dune,* was one
of the most notorious commercial and critical disasters of all
time. The one after that, *Blue Velvet,* became one of the decade's
touchstone works of art. *Time* magazine put him on the cover
in 1990, the "Czar of Bizarre" behind *Twin Peaks;* the show was
canceled a few months later.

Lynch won the Palme d'Or, the prestigious top prize at
Cannes, in 1990 for *Wild at Heart;* at the festival two years later,
Twin Peaks: Fire Walk with Me was booed and he was heckled
at his press conference. Next came *Lost Highway,* widely considered his most perplexing movie to date. Short of critical raves
to choose from, the distributor used a Siskel and Ebert slam —
TWO THUMBS DOWN! — in the ads. The follow-up, *The
Straight Story,* rated G and released by Disney, was universally
deemed the most accessible film of his career.

When ABC, the network that axed *Twin Peaks,* nixed his
proposed series, *Mulholland Drive,* he turned the unfinished pilot episode into a stand-alone movie, which earned him his best
reviews since *Blue Velvet* and another Academy Award nomination. His response to this unlikely triumph was to insist on
more artistic freedom, which he achieved by renouncing celluloid for good. ("Film is like a dinosaur in a tar pit.") He shot *Inland Empire* on a cheap, consumer-grade digital-video camera,
in much the same fashion as *Eraserhead:* piecemeal over several
years. He also self-distributed the film, and in one promotional
gambit, he parked himself on a Hollywood street corner with a
FOR YOUR CONSIDERATION banner and a live cow.

Lynch has been a renaissance man all his working life: He
drew a weekly cartoon strip called *The Angriest Dog in the
World* for a full decade and has always found time for painting,
photography, furniture design, music, and more. His studio art
has reached its widest audience in his later years, with large exhibitions in Paris (*The Air Is on Fire* at the Fondation Cartier in
2007) and at his old student stomping grounds in Philadelphia

(*The Unified Field* at the Pennsylvania Academy of the Fine Arts in 2014). He has also released two albums, *Crazy Clown Time* (2011) and *The Big Dream* (2013); put in a very funny guest performance as a terse showbiz sage on Louis C. K.'s anti-sitcom *Louie;* sold his own line of organic coffee; partnered with the shoe designer Christian Louboutin on a touring exhibition featuring shadowy photos of female nudes in red-lacquered fetishistic stilettos; designed a members-only nightclub in Paris called Silencio, named after and modeled on the after-hours spot in *Mulholland Drive;* and directed a tour documentary for Duran Duran and a fifteen-minute promo for Christian Dior starring Marion Cotillard, just to name a few of his many ventures. A vocal proponent of Transcendental Meditation, he has also been stumping on behalf of the David Lynch Foundation for Consciousness-Based Education and World Peace, promoting meditation in schools, meeting world leaders, and conducting lectures with an unlikely troupe of fellow meditators, including the actor Russell Brand, the physicist John Hagelin, and the 1960s folkie Donovan.

Lynch's career is a series of ups and downs, filled with meteoric rises, spectacular collapses, unexpected detours, and long bouts of inactivity. Looked at another way, it is also a model of constancy, a testament to a single-mindedness that verges on the autistic.

The first time I asked David Lynch if he could define the word "Lynchian," he changed the subject. This was in the fall of 2001, shortly before the release of *Mulholland Drive,* and as he often does when invited to reflect on his own work, he reverted to homespun philosophizing. "It means different things to different people," he said. "You know, there's an expression that I heard from my friend Charlie"—he was referring to Charlie Lutes, a TM lecturer who was the first person to sign up with the Maharishi in the continental United States—"'Keep your eye on the doughnut, and not on the hole.'" A concept like "Lynchian," he continued, is "more like the hole. If I start thinking about that, it's so dangerous."

Despite his protestations, and despite having made only ten feature films, Lynch has spent much of his working life in the pantheon of the eponymous, among the very small group of artists who have become household adjectives through the singular force and character of their work. In Lynch's case, this is a testament not just to his uniqueness but also to the difficulty of accounting for that uniqueness. If "Kafkaesque" implies an atmosphere of ominous illogic and "Borgesian" suggests a garden of forking paths, if "Capraesque" connotes feel-good optimism and "Felliniesque" conjures carnival-like fantasy, "Lynchian" means — well, this is where things get both tricky and interesting.

The paradox of the Lynchian sensibility is that it is at once easy to recognize and hard to define. The quaint small towns of *Blue Velvet* and *Twin Peaks* seem indelibly Lynchian, but so do the haunted Los Angeles nightscapes of *Lost Highway* and *Mulholland Drive* and the two-lane highways of *Wild at Heart* and *The Straight Story*. To anyone with a passing familiarity with his films — to anyone, in other words, with a modicum of pop-culture literacy — any number of sights and sounds will seem instantly Lynchian. A road at night. A woman's crimson lips. Red drapes and a spotlit stage. A situation can turn Lynchian before our eyes, from a flicker of a lightbulb or a swelling rumble on the sound track, from an untimely pause or a charge of déjà vu. But Lynch is more than the sum of his effects. A catalog of weirdness fails to account for the irreducible strangeness and power of the films, or the fascination they exert.

Filmmakers as different as Tim Burton, Quentin Tarantino, the Coen brothers, and Harmony Korine have been called Lynchian. And the concept is by no means confined to cinema. The self-reflexive fictions of the Chilean novelist Roberto Bolaño and the twisty, mythology-driven television series *Lost* have been termed Lynchian. A curator of a Paris retrospective devoted to the photojournalist Don McCullin spoke of "*une ambiance lynchienne*" in one of McCullin's images, of the Berlin Wall under construction in 1960. Bruce Springsteen has described the small-town America of his youth as "very Lynchian": "Everything was there, but underneath, everything was rumbling." The British record industry veteran Alan McGee came to the defense of Susan Boyle, the *Britain's Got Talent* contestant turned Internet sensation and best-selling middle-of-the-road balladeer, calling her music Lynchian — for being "eerily detached to an almost tragic degree." A Louis Vuitton designer described his 2011 line of men's cardigans and corduroys — Amish influenced, with "a hint of strangeness" and a splash of "motel red" — as Lynchian.

The more widely its manifestations range, the more difficult it is to distill the Lynchian to its essence. A common trap is to fall back on the vaguest of terms: feelings, impressions, moods. But vagueness, of course, is a central quality of the Lynchian, tied as it is to ineffable notions — the sublime, the uncanny, the abject — and to the uncontainable sensations that define Lynch's best work: abysmal terror, piercing beauty, convulsive sorrow. David Foster Wallace, the most obsessively precise of writers, ventured a definition in his essay "David Lynch Keeps His Head." Lynchian, he wrote, is "a particular kind of irony where the very macabre and the very mundane combine in such a way as to reveal the former's perpetual containment within the latter." Even so, Wallace acknowledged that it is one of those concepts that is "ultimately definable only ostensively — i.e., we know it when we see it."

The term is bandied about so frequently by now that it is simply, more often than not, a synonym for "weird." But that overuse attests to the curiously central place that Lynch occupies in the cultural consciousness, despite his relatively scant filmography. The singularity of his work is a big part of it — as is the sheer improbability of his career, the sense that he has always been an anomaly. Born in 1946, Lynch is an exact contemporary of Steven Spielberg. *Eraserhead* had its premiere just two months before George Lucas's *Star Wars*. Lynch belongs to the generation that also includes Francis Ford Coppola, Martin Scorsese, and Terrence Malick (his classmate at the American Film Institute). But unlike most of his peers, Lynch reshaped American cinema without ever being absorbed into the Hollywood establishment. Quite the opposite, in fact: Lynch's signal achievement is the degree to which he has infiltrated the mainstream with an essentially avant-garde aesthetic.

A populist experimental filmmaker, Lynch has only grown freer and more radical with age. He has also become more of a personality. Few other film directors exist as figures in the public consciousness. The exceptions, from Hitchcock to Herzog to Tarantino, frequently insert their outsize personas into their movies. Lynch rarely appears in his films, which are not confessional in any obvious way, but they cultivate a psychological intimacy all the same. They give the impression of having been mainlined straight from his unconscious, and they seek to activate something in ours. It is hard to know how to take them except personally.

One of the first video recordings of a David Lynch interview dates from 1979. The twenty-minute black-and-white segment was produced for a television course at the University of California, Los Angeles, and conducted at one of the locations that constituted the barren wasteland of *Eraserhead:* the oil fields of the Los Angeles Basin, where rigs and derricks once loomed over the urban landscape. (Crude oil is still big business in Southern California, but the signs of industry are now largely hidden from view, absorbed into daily life. This particular site now houses the colossal Beverly Center shopping mall, where drilling operations continue to this day, behind a wall next to Bloomingdale's.)

This was the moment of Lynch's first brush with cult fame: *Eraserhead* was a year into its three-year run at the Nu-Art Theatre on Santa Monica Boulevard. Against a backdrop of hulking tanks and rusted pipes, an eager student reporter named Tom Christie directs questions to Lynch and his cinematographer Frederick Elmes. The thirty-three-year-old Lynch, in a voice so flat and nasal it verges on cartoonish, enthuses about all the "neat areas" "down in the tanks," explaining that he found the location while driving by one day: "I think this place is beautiful . . . if you look at it right." He directs the camera's attention to a blotch on the ground: the remains of a cat procured from a veterinarian for use in the film that "got covered with tar and preserved itself."

Citing the vague tagline that describes *Eraserhead* as "A Dream of Dark and Troubling Things," Christie asks Lynch: "Would you like to expound on that a little?" "No," the filmmaker replies immediately, shaking his head and smiling. Christie reads from a review that likens the movie to both a dream and a nightmare. Lynch reacts with puzzlement. "I'm not sure I know what that means," he says, before conceding, "That's a fine statement, you know?"

Affable despite his elusiveness, Lynch seems less to be stonewalling than striving to verbalize daunting concepts with a vocabulary that might politely be termed basic. *Eraserhead* was "a real, definite thing in my head," he says. "It's not just like thrown-together abstract; it's meant to be abstract." Christie points out an apparent incongruity: Lynch the family man and Lynch the creator of the dark, weird *Eraserhead*. "I'm not all that strange, really," Lynch responds. "And also, beneath a lot of times a calm exterior is the subconscious, right? And that's where everyone has their — well, not little — the denizens of the deep and all that." He proposes a working theory of filmmaking as world making: "No matter how weird something is, no matter how strange the world is that you're making a film about, it's got to be a certain way. Once you see how that is, it can't be another way or it's not that place anymore. It breaks the mood or the feeling." Finally he gets in a good closing one-liner, explaining his decision to cast the unknown Jack Nance and not a name actor: "If you're going into the netherworld, you don't want to go in with Chuck Heston."

The David Lynch of today is, in many ways, not so far removed from this pale, polite young man, doing his best not to squirm under interrogation. The floppy hair would later swoop up into a signature quiff. The unfussy attire — a light shirt and zip-up jacket in the video — would be formalized as a uniform: khaki slacks, a slightly rumpled black suit jacket, and, most distinctive of all, a white shirt primly buttoned to the top. (This getup has not escaped the attention of men's magazines. *GQ* has called the no-tie, buttoned-up style "the David Lynch look." *Esquire* went so far as to dub the filmmaker an accidental fashion icon: "David Lynch dresses badly, but he gets away with it and you can't.")

In person Lynch projects niceness. He has kindly eyes, a soft-featured handsomeness, an air of corn-fed good cheer. He has often sought out these very qualities in his actors, most notably Kyle MacLachlan, who bears a physical resemblance to him. But there is also something a bit peculiar about Lynch's niceness — a heightened, golly-gee, stuck-in-the-1950s folksiness that some people think must be a put-on. The biography he typically uses for press releases consists of four words: "Eagle Scout, Missoula, Montana." Whether innate or cultivated or both, the picture of David Lynch the straight-arrow square is striking for the obvious contrast with the darkness and extremity of the work, its obsession with grotesquerie and depravity. In view of the work, in fact, Lynch's mild-mannered calm can seem somewhat creepy.

This is the contradiction—David Lynch the all-American weirdo—that defines how we think about him. Mel Brooks is said to have called him "Jimmy Stewart from Mars" (the quote is also attributed to producer Stuart Cornfeld) and David Foster Wallace described his voice as "Jimmy Stewart on acid."

That voice has become more caricatured over the years, even the subject of self-parody. Most of us know it from Lynch's recurring cameo as the hard-of-hearing FBI bureau chief Gordon Cole in *Twin Peaks,* whose foghorn delivery only slightly exaggerates Lynch's speaking voice. So much about Lynch's fraught relationship with language is summed up in that voice, in its unnervingly high volume and halting cadences. It's clear from the 1979 footage—and from almost every interview he has done since—that words do not come easily to him. Both Lynch and his first wife, Peggy Reavey (née Lentz), have referred to his "preverbal" years, a phase that lasted into his early twenties, when he had a hard time stringing even more than a few words together. In his early short film *The Alphabet,* verbal learning is a source of dread: A young girl is terrorized by the letters of the alphabet as she sleeps.

In Lynch's own speech—and in the speech patterns of his films, with their gnomic pronouncements and recurring mantras—the impression is of language used less for meaning than for sound. To savor the thingness of words is to move away from their imprisoning nature. Lynch has said, more than once, that he had to "learn to talk," and his very particular, somewhat limited vocabulary seems in many ways an outgrowth of his aesthetic. In keeping with his interest in the intangible, he has a curious, syntactically awkward fondness for abstract nouns: "When you do something that works you have a happiness." "It's such a sadness that you think you've seen a film on your fucking telephone." If his films swing between extreme moods, so too does the tenor of his conversation, especially when he's discussing his work. Great ideas are "beautiful" and "thrilling" and make you "fall in love"; when the creative process is impeded, it's a "terrible thing" that can feel "like death." (What Lynch, a prodigious coffee drinker, lacks in eloquence, he generally makes up for with caffeinated enthusiasm.)

It is not uncommon for artists to believe that their art should speak for itself. But Lynch's aphasia is born of a protectiveness that verges on superstition. Words for him are not just reductive, they are dangerous, anathema to his view of art as fundamentally enigmatic. He says often that his films should leave "room to dream." To decode a film, to proffer interpretations, to divulge the source of an idea—all these simply mean less room and fewer possible dreams. Called upon to describe his films, Lynch typically gives the most minimal one-liners: *Eraserhead* is "a dream of dark and troubling things"; *Inland Empire* is the story of "a woman in trouble." From as far back as *Eraserhead,* he was careful to seed his burgeoning legend with mysteries: He has never revealed what he used to create the movie's mutant baby (the most popular rumor holds that it was a calf fetus). He has also claimed that *Eraserhead* came together in his head when he chanced upon a sentence in the Bible, while pointedly refusing to specify which one.

Lynch has not exactly been mute on the subject of his art and creative process. He has repeatedly advanced an almost mystical notion of ideas as having a life of their own, independent of the artist and waiting to be plucked from the ether. Sometimes he likens himself to a radio, tuning in inspiration on odd frequencies. More often he compares ideas to fish, swimming in an ocean of possibilities. The fullest illustration of these concepts can be found in his 2006 book *Catching the Big Fish: Meditation, Consciousness, and Creativity,* which combines scattered autobiographical anecdotes, creativity-boosting tips, and quotes from the Bhagavad Gita and the Upanishads. Somewhere between Lynch's own teenage bible, Robert Henri's *The Art Spirit,* and self-help propaganda, the book consists of many extremely short chapters in which Lynch typically describes a problem he has faced — anger, stress, writer's block — and in every case recommends meditation as a solution. There are a few resonant bits of wisdom ("There's a safety in thinking in a diner") and some instances of accidental poetry ("every single thing that is a thing"), but mostly, the writing is robotically declarative ("I love the French." "I love dream logic.") and so repetitive that it all but induces a trancelike stupor. Reading *Catching the Big Fish,* you're reminded that the film critic Pauline Kael once called Lynch a genius naif and that David Foster Wallace, reporting from the set of *Lost Highway,* noted, "It's hard to tell if he's a genius or an idiot." All of which is in line with the Lynch persona as we have come to know it: the primitive artist of our most modern art.

While Lynch may take a hard stand against interpretation, his interpreters are legion. Despite his own reticence, there exists a proliferating cottage industry of Lynch studies, from the casual yet obsessive efforts of cultists to the more strenuous heavy lifting of scholars. No other filmmaker, save perhaps Alfred Hitchcock, has had his body of work so closely and extensively psychoanalyzed. And no wonder: Almost all of Lynch's films are vivid illustrations of the basic instincts of Eros and Thanatos. His characters exhibit symptoms that might have come from psychiatric manuals: Is Dorothy Vallens, the battered heroine of *Blue Velvet,* suffering from Stockholm syndrome? Has Fred Madison, the possible wife killer of *Lost Highway,* entered another dimension or a psychogenic fugue state? Lynch, for his part, professes ignorance when it comes to psychotherapy. He once went to a psychiatrist and, after the first session, asked if the process might inhibit his creativity. The shrink said yes and Lynch never returned.

Lynch has also proved irresistible to the academic discipline of cinema studies. As it became institutionalized in the 1960s and 1970s, film theory borrowed concepts from semiotics and linguistics, feminism and psychoanalysis. By the time *Blue Velvet* became a cultural event in 1986, postmodernism was a thriving field of study and a dominant mode of academic discourse. Rich in contradiction and mysterious in its effects, with a plot that vividly and literally dramatizes such Freudian concepts as the primal scene and the Oedipus complex, *Blue Velvet* opened the floodgates for Lynch studies. For many big guns of critical theory it was a dream text for analysis. The Marxist critic Fredric Jameson characterized it as a quintessential postmodern film for its nostalgic attraction to a past that never existed. Feminist theorists examined it in terms of gender and power relations. Some attacked it for misogyny; others defended it as a multi-layered complication of the patriarchal "male gaze." The first book-length scholarly study of Lynch emerged in 1993, and dozens more have surfaced since. Conferences have been convened and countless papers published, holding up a myriad of analytical prisms to his films, from Lacanian psychoanalytic theory to quantum physics. Any number of Lynchian tics and tropes have been pored over for possible clues, from the prevalence of disability and prosthetic limbs in his films to his evident fondness for midcentury design.

Lynch sees his movies as worlds to inhabit; for devoted fans, they are often environments that encourage lingering. *Twin Peaks* took event television to new heights, inspiring coffee-and-cherry-pie viewing parties and fostering a community of avid interpreters, from doctoral students dissecting "the semiotics of cobbler," as *Premiere* magazine snidely put it, to a zine, *Wrapped in Plastic,* that ran seventy-five issues, until September 2005. (Its title referred to the state of the homecoming queen and resident ghost of *Twin Peaks,* Laura Palmer, when found washed up on the shores of a lake.) *Twin Peaks* was addictive not just for its tease of a drawn-out murder mystery or Lynchian oddities like a backward-talking dwarf, but also because it offered the opportunity to step into a fully imagined Pacific Northwest logging town, filled equally with unknown terrors and the comforts of the everyday: "a completely furnished world," as the Italian philosopher Umberto Eco said, describing one precondition for a film to attain cult status. Lynch's most iconic works are invitations to immersion. For its original viewers *Eraserhead* was nothing if not a ritualistic experience, a midnight movie that defined its era. *Blue Velvet* enjoyed a healthy afterlife on home video, where viewers of an impressionable age still encounter it both as a revelation and a rite of passage. *Mulholland Drive* prompted much head-scratching, but a sizable contingent of fans seized on it as a puzzle to be solved and, as numerous websites suggest, have spent untold hours untangling its narrative threads and mapping its larger cosmology.

Lynch's work so readily lends itself to analysis in large part because of its taste for extremes. Most of his films set up stark contrasts—or queasy confluences—of good and evil. In both literal and figurative senses they depict light fading into darkness and in turn emerging into light. Plots are mirrored, characters twinned (often in blond-brunette iterations). Things happen twice, or they cancel each other out. His films are rife with the binary oppositions that underlie our dominant ways of thinking: an ideal fit for the constellation of dualisms and dialectics that are fundamental organizing principles for any number of philosophies, religions, and systems of knowledge. But if Lynch has inspired so many interpreters—and if so many of them are so persuasive—why does he still seem like a mystery yet to be cracked? The more theories there are, the better they fit, the more stubbornly elusive Lynch can seem, as if you could see him through almost any lens and come away none the wiser.

2

Three Ideas of America

GOOD TIMES ON *Our Street* is the title of a once popular children's book, first published in January 1945.
An elementary reader in the Dick and Jane style, it
chronicles the exploits of apple-cheeked siblings Jim and Judy,
first seen alongside their white picket fence as they catch sight
of a merry-go-round that has been installed on their tree-lined
street. There are a few pulse-quickening escapades — a bicycle
accident, a baby bear escaped from the circus — but what pre-
vails is a kid's-eye view of neighborly coziness: encounters with
friendly authority figures and upbeat initiations into the adult
world of work. Several sylvan interludes include stories about
bears hibernating in winter and the robins that herald the ar-
rival of spring.

Good Times, which appeared as part of a Macmillan series of
readers called Today's Work-Play Books, was a staple in elementary schools across Cold War America. For David Lynch, who
encountered it as a six-year-old in Spokane, Washington, its
cheerful depictions of small-town contentment remain the burnished epitome — the literal story-book version — of his 1950s
upbringing: "Mostly what I saw was very happy," he said in 1982,
responding to an interviewer who wondered if *Eraserhead* was
an expression of childhood anxieties. "It was good times on our
street."

• • •

"It's morning again in America," goes the soothing opening line of Ronald Reagan's best-known campaign commercial (titled "Prouder, Stronger, Better"). An uplifting paean to the ideals of marriage, family, hard work, and home ownership, this dense, minute-long montage of everyday Americans doing profoundly American things saturated the airwaves during the election season of 1984, with the economy on an upswing and patriotic sentiment cresting in anticipation of the Soviet-boycotted Los Angeles Summer Olympics. Strings swell on the sound track as a narrator trumpets low interest and inflation rates. The gauzy images promise good times on every street: A boy bikes along a sidewalk on his paper route; a nuclear family proudly carries a rolled-up rug into their picket-fenced house; children look skyward as a firefighter raises the Stars and Stripes.

More than fifty-four million Americans voted for Reagan in his landslide reelection over Walter Mondale that year. One of them was David Lynch, who was also twice a guest at the Reagan White House. Lynch typically avoids political statements and has described himself as a libertarian; he directed a 2000 campaign commercial for Natural Law Party candidate John Hagelin, a fellow meditator, and voiced his support for the 2012 reelection of Barack Obama, albeit strictly in terms of a deep antipathy toward Mitt Romney ("If you just rearrange a few letters, Romney becomes R MONEY. I believe Mitt Romney wants to get his Mitts on R Money"). The few times Lynch explained his support of Reagan, he provided entirely vague or superficial reasons: "I liked this one speech he read early on, at a convention." "I mostly liked that he carried a wind of old Hollywood, of a cowboy and a brush-clearer."

Blue Velvet, the 1986 film that turned David Lynch from an intriguing oddball director into a brand-name auteur, has one of the most indelible opening sequences of all time. We see a white picket fence fronted by red roses and a bright blue sky overhead as Bobby Vinton croons the doleful title song (his 1963 hit cover of Tony Bennett's 1951 standard). If the Reagan ad of two years earlier had filtered very similar images through a soft-focus lens, *Blue Velvet* gives them a lush, picture-book intensity, heightening the patriotic colors to the point of radioactivity. In slow motion, a beaming fireman, a Dalmatian by his side, waves from a passing fire truck; a crossing guard holding a bright red stop sign beckons to a procession of happy children.

This dementedly sunny idyll doesn't last long. A middle-aged man in a Panama hat and sunglasses, watering his lawn, gets his hose snagged on a branch and is overcome by some kind of seizure or perhaps an insect bite, clutching his neck as he falls to the ground. Garden-hose mishaps are as old as cinema itself: For one of their first films, *The Sprinkler Sprinkled,* from 1895, the year of the medium's birth, the Lumière brothers turned their newly invented *cinématographe* on a gardener who gets completely drenched as a result of a practical joke. It's often cited as the first example of a film comedy. Lynch's scenario is not quite slapstick but it has an absurdist pathos all its own. The man is still clutching the hose as he writhes and grimaces on his back. A yelping dog laps at the spray from the nozzle, and an uncomprehending toddler wanders toward the commotion. Lynch's camera moves beyond this awful spectacle, pushing past the wet blades of grass to reveal, in gleaming close-up, a swarm of pitch-black beetles, as their ominous roar fills the sound track. Here, distilled down to a couple of minutes, is the story that *Blue Velvet* will tell: one about order and its destruction.

Blue Velvet is a coming-of-age tale, an off-key song of innocence and experience. Summoned home to small-town Lumberton to visit his hospitalized father (the unfortunate man on the lawn), fresh-faced college student Jeffrey Beaumont (Kyle Mac-Lachlan) discovers a severed ear in an abandoned field. The ear is a portal, a rabbit hole, into Lumberton's — and Jeffrey's own — heart of darkness. Chasing clues through a mystery that he sometimes seems to be willing into existence, Jeffrey finds himself torn, as often happens in a Lynch film, between a blonde and a brunette: Sandy Williams (Laura Dern), the wholesome daughter of the local detective, and Dorothy Vallens (Isabella Rossellini), a torch-singing damsel in distress whose husband and son have been kidnapped. The man holding Dorothy's family hostage is Frank Booth (Dennis Hopper), a maniac with a taste for rough sex and warped mind games who enters the film with a force that borders the occult.

As Lynch more than once reminds us, this is a horror movie, a story about good and evil, set in the bosom of small-town America but resonating on a cosmic scale. Parked opposite a church the night after witnessing Frank's ritualistic brutalization of Dorothy, Jeffrey turns to Sandy and, practically in tears, delivers an anguished outburst that inevitably prompts audience laughter: "Why are there people like Frank? Why is there so much trouble in this world?" Sincerity can rip open a Lynch film as decisively as dread. Backlit by the glow of illuminated stained glass, accompanied by a faint church organ on the sound track, Sandy recounts a dream she had the night she met Jeffrey: "In the dream, there was our world, and the world was dark because there weren't any robins, and the robins represented love. And for the longest time there was just this darkness, and all of a sudden thousands of robins were set free and they flew down and brought this blinding light of love. And it seemed like that love would be the only thing that would make any difference. And it did." Breaking from her childlike reverie, Sandy turns to Jeffrey: "So I guess it means that there is trouble until the robins come."

Blue Velvet ends with the apparent fulfillment of Sandy's dream. Jeffrey shoots Frank dead, saving Dorothy, in effect turning her from a whore back into a mother, and allowing Jeffrey and Sandy to resume their chaste courtship. But the film's conclusion — like its opening — has the heightened, brittle feel of a hallucination: an idyll waiting to be shattered. In the family gathering that ends the movie, Jeffrey, Sandy, and Jeffrey's aunt Barbara look out the kitchen window at a robin perched on a branch with a bug in its mouth. The most disconcerting thing about the scene is that the bird appears to be mechanical (the insect is not). "I could never do that," an appalled Aunt Barbara says, as she pops an unidentifiable object into her own mouth.

The story of the robins in *Good Times on Our Street,* the book that so enchanted the six-year-old David Lynch, makes no specific mention of their diet, perhaps so as not to appall its young readers. But there in plain sight, at the bottom of page 113, is an image of tenderness and revulsion, hunger and need: A robin with a wriggling worm in its beak, suspended over the open mouths of a nestful of baby robins.

3

Big Sky Country

D AVID KEITH LYNCH was born on January 20, 1946, in Missoula, the second-largest city in the northwestern state of Montana. He was the first child of Donald and Edwina "Sunny" Lynch, who met on a biology field trip as students at Duke University in Durham, North Carolina — he was studying for a master's degree in forestry; she majored in English and foreign languages. They both served in the navy during World War II and were married in January 1945 at the naval chapel on Mare Island in California. After the war, the couple moved to Donald's native Montana, where he started a job with the U.S. Forest Service, the agency of the Department of Agriculture that Theodore Roosevelt established to manage the country's forest reserves.

Missoula, Montana, is where the forest service's northern region has its headquarters, but Donald, who worked as a research scientist, was transferred frequently. David was only two months old when the family left Missoula for Sandpoint, Idaho, where his brother, John, was born. They moved two years later to Spokane, Washington, where the Lynches had their third child, Martha, and then to Boise, Idaho, where David attended elementary and junior high school. When David was fourteen, the family moved again, to Alexandria, Virginia, where he finished high school.

He may have left Montana as an infant, but Big Sky Country, with its vast open spaces, lakes, and mountains, occupies a central place in David Lynch's self-image ("Eagle Scout, Missoula, Montana"). Missoula, a town of about twenty-five thousand in the 1940s, was a pit stop on the Lewis and Clark expedition and not far from what was once the world's largest lumber mill. Surrounded by wilderness in all directions, it sits at the hub of five valleys; looming to the east are the city's signature twin peaks of Mount Jumbo and Mount Sentinel. Lynch's paternal roots run deep in this region: Donald came from a line of Montana ranchers, and David has spoken fondly of his grandfather Ernest, a wheat rancher who drove Buicks and wore polished cowboy boots and string ties with his western suits. Donald and Sunny eventually settled in Riverside, California, but also kept a house in Whitefish, Montana. In *Catching the Big Fish,* Lynch refers to himself as "just a guy from Missoula, Montana," which he calls "not the surrealist capital of the world." But, he adds, "you could be anywhere and see a kind of strangeness in how the world is these days, or have a certain way of looking at things." In *Twin Peaks,* when Leland Palmer, revealed as his daughter's killer, attacks the dead Laura's look-alike cousin, Madeleine, smashing her face into a picture frame, he ushers her into oblivion with the words: "You're going back to Missoula, Montana!"

"There are many Lumbertons in America," Lynch has said, and he grew up in several of them. Donald's job sent the Lynches all over northwestern timber country — from one lumber town to another, always on the edges of deep, dark forests — and David would ride along with his father in his pickup truck on work expeditions. "I spent a lot of time out in the woods, building fires," Lynch recalled in a 1987 interview. (The adolescent David's pyromanic tendencies got him arrested in Boise when he and a few friends tossed a homemade pipe bomb into their school's swimming pool.) Donald worked with diseased trees and insect infestation, which may account for his son's childhood fascination with tactile organic matter and the cycle of life and decomposition: Lynch began incorporating dead bugs into his paintings while in high school.

Speaking of his childhood, Lynch has offered several variations on this quote, which in imagery and mood perfectly matches the opening of *Blue Velvet:* "It was beautiful old houses, tree-lined streets, the milkman, building forts, lots and lots of friends. It was a dream world, those droning airplanes, blue skies, picket fences, green grass, cherry trees — Middle America the way it was supposed to be." But there was also one particular cherry tree in the Lynches' backyard in Spokane, which had "this pitch oozing out, some of it black, some of it yellow, and there were millions of red ants racing all over the sticky pitch, all over the tree. So you see, there's this beautiful world and you just look a little bit closer, and it's all red ants." Elsewhere he has recast his childhood memories in explicitly cinematic terms: "I saw life in one extreme closeup shot — in one, for instance, of saliva mingled with blood — or in long shots of a peaceful environment."

The first movie Lynch remembers seeing, at a drive-in with his parents, was *Wait Till the Sun Shines, Nellie,* a 1952 Technicolor ode to small-town wholesomeness by Henry King. The one image from the movie he has repeatedly cited as an indelible memory is of a button getting stuck in a girl's throat — perhaps prefiguring the esophageal trauma in *Six Men Getting Sick* and the choking seizures that befall the hero's girlfriend and her mother in *Eraserhead.* In Boise, the Lynches lived down the street from a movie house, the Vista Theatre (Jeffrey, in *Blue Velvet,* finds the ear in a field "there behind Vista"), where he watched sci-fi monster movies and Delmer Daves teen romances.

The Lynch household was, by all accounts, as normal as could be: Donald and Sunny were churchgoing Presbyterians who didn't drink or smoke, and aside from his brief flirtation with bomb making, David was a well-liked kid who adjusted without much difficulty to the family's constant moving. But much like Jeffrey in *Blue Velvet,* Lynch recognized — or perhaps hoped — that there was more to his apple-pie existence than met the eye. "I knew it as a kid but I couldn't find the proof," he told Chris Rodley in the book-length interview *Lynch on Lynch*. "It was just a feeling. There is goodness in blue skies and flowers, but another force — a wild pain and decay — also accompanies everything." He told another interviewer that "smiles were pretty much all I saw," but he also called them "strange smiles," "smiles of the way the world could be or should be." He remembers wishing that his parents, who never fought, would get into an argument. Domestic life was cozy but claustrophobic, even ominous, he told Rodley: "The home is a place where things can go wrong."

Lynch's rendition of his childhood — always in the Kodachrome hyperreality of the *Blue Velvet* prologue, picture-perfect with an undercurrent of unease — calls to mind a line from *Lost Highway*. "I like to remember things my own way," says the Bill Pullman character, explaining why he hates camcorders. "How I remembered them. Not necessarily how they happened." When Lynch came upon the Henry King film on television in the 1980s, he changed the channel — so as not to risk encountering something that contradicted his memory of it.

Neither jock nor nerd, the teenage David swam, played baseball, and, to please his father, joined the Boy Scouts. In his Eagle Scout uniform, on his fifteenth birthday, he helped to seat VIPs in the bleachers outside the White House at John F. Kennedy's inauguration. He likes to tell the story of seeing Eisenhower and Kennedy gliding by in one limo, followed by Lyndon Johnson and Richard Nixon in another: four consecutive U.S. presidents in a row. At high school in Alexandria, already a fiscal conservative, he ran for class treasurer under the slogan "Save with Dave." (He lost.) He and a girlfriend were voted cutest couple and pictured in their yearbook on a bicycle for two. But he was also, by his own admission, a somewhat fearful, mildly agoraphobic young man: "I had a touch of that disease where you're afraid to go out of the house," he told an interviewer in 1992. Sometime in his teens, Lynch developed the habit of buttoning his shirt to the very top and even wearing two or three ties: defense mechanism disguised as eccentric fashion statement. "If my collarbone gets wind on it, it feels strange," he once said. "I'm very insecure, and it makes me feel better to have something around my neck."

Lynch remembers *Wait Till the Sun Shines, Nellie* for its choking scene, but the movie — "a mawkishly sentimental tribute . . . to the dubious felicities of living in an American small town," per the *New York Times* review — also sums up the polarities of Lynch's America. A young husband brings his city-slicker wife to a small town where he opens a barber shop (one of the bedrock institutions depicted in *Good Times on Our Street*); she leaves for Chicago mid-movie and promptly gets herself killed.

It was Sunny Lynch, a New Yorker, who introduced her son to the big, bad city. In the woods of his childhood, David would spend hours fixating on the sap and insects on diseased trees as if watching television. Visiting his maternal grandparents in Brooklyn, he realized that the city contained its own sort of decay. Lynch has described cities as places where "everything is falling faster than we can clean it or build it or make it right." He experienced the New York City subway as a Dantean inferno: "I felt I was really going down into hell . . . It was the total fear of the unknown — the wind from those trains, the sounds, the smells, and the different light and mood — that was really special in a traumatic way." As the young David saw it, the strange moods of the city also encouraged strange behavior: His grandfather owned an apartment building in Park Slope with no kitchens, and Lynch remembers seeing one of its residents cooking an egg on an iron ("That really worried me").

At the still impressionable age of nineteen, David Lynch moved to Philadelphia, an epicenter of urban blight at the time, and a city that he would later memorialize as a veritable Gomorrah: "a very sick, twisted, violent, fear-ridden, decadent, decaying place."

4

City of Industry

AFTER HIGH SCHOOL, Lynch, determined to become a painter, enrolled at the School of the Museum of Fine Arts in Boston. Both he and his best friend, Jack Fisk, who opted for the Cooper Union in New York City, were disappointed after their first years, so in the summer of 1965, they set off for Europe, which seemed to hold more opportunities to lead the "art life" — for one, the prospect of studying with the Austrian expressionist painter Oskar Kokoschka (to whom Lynch had a connection through school in Boston). "We were like dreamers," Fisk told me in a 2007 interview. But the reality didn't match up to their dreams. Kokoschka wasn't in Salzburg when they arrived. Adrift in Paris, they debated between Portugal (Fisk's choice) and Greece (Lynch's, because a girl he liked was visiting family there). They flipped a coin; Lynch won. A three-day trip to Athens aboard the Orient Express resulted in more disappointment: Lynch's potential love interest had returned to the States. No romantic incentive, no artistic inspiration to speak of, and rapidly depleting funds, partly because of Lynch's appetite for imported Marlboros, an expensive habit on a backpacker budget — they lasted all of fifteen days in Europe before flying home.

Back in Alexandria, Lynch continued to paint, but his father wouldn't support him if he wasn't in school, so Lynch took a series of jobs — none of which he kept for very long — at an architecture firm, an art-supply store, and a frame shop (where he was demoted to janitor after scratching a frame). Fisk, meanwhile, had transferred to the Pennsylvania Academy of the Fine Arts (PAFA) in Philadelphia and urged Lynch to join him — they were both also called for an army physical at the same time, which made college a more appealing option. Lynch applied and was accepted in late 1965, in time for the winter semester.

On New Year's Eve 1965, Lynch moved in with Fisk, who was renting a run-down apartment on the corner of North Thirteenth and Wood Streets, in the heart of an active industrial zone crisscrossed by freight lines, opposite the concrete-and-steel Heid Building, which once produced accordion envelopes. The rent was dirt cheap, and it was a short walk from the academy's main building on Broad Street, but their living quarters offered little in the way of comfort and amenities. The building was due to be razed and in a state of chronic neglect; some of the windows were missing, which let in the snow and howling wind during the harsh Northeast winters. Fisk remembers them having to rig an old coffee pot to serve as a water heater.

Past its manufacturing heyday, Philadelphia in the mid-1960s was riven by crime and poverty and, in the wake of race riots in north Philadelphia in 1964, ethnic tensions. Lynch and Fisk lived next door to a greasy spoon called Pop's Diner, and Lynch, who tended to sleep through the day and work through the night, would make sure to wake up in time to get a coffee at Pop's before it closed at 6 p.m. At the diner he befriended the workers at the cavernous city morgue, kitty-corner from their apartment. Fisk recalls that the morgue employees would invite Lynch over "to see things like the parts room, where the pieces would go if they hadn't found the whole body." It's not a stretch to connect the sights Lynch encountered at the Philly morgue — the city's murder rate rose steeply through the 1960s, peaking in the early 1970s — to some of the images in his films, starting with the severed ear in *Blue Velvet*. Lynch once described the body bags that he would see on the sidewalk across the street, unzipped and sagging after being hosed down, as "smiling bags of death" — in *Twin Peaks,* which opens with the appearance of Laura Palmer's plastic-swaddled corpse, one of Agent Cooper's dream-world premonitions is of "a man in a smiling bag."

In his first year at the academy, Lynch started dating a fellow student and painter named Peggy Lentz. They were married in 1967, bought a three-story row house for $3,500 in the Fairmount neighborhood that same year, and had a daughter, Jennifer, in April 1968. Lynch's new neighborhood was less grimy and sooty, but it was no safer. Their house was broken into three times, twice when they were in it; their windows were shot out, their car was stolen, and a kid was shot to death on their block. Lynch later spoke in interviews of violent episodes and images that he and Peggy witnessed in those years that seared themselves into his mind: carjackings, gang attacks, chalk body outlines.

Even in 1987, seventeen years after he left Philadelphia for Los Angeles, the mere memory of this formative environment was transporting: "I just have to think of Philadelphia now and I get ideas, I hear the wind, and I'm off into the darkness somewhere." Attuned no doubt to Philadelphia's central role in his personal mythology, Lynch himself has pointed out that his Thirteenth Street apartment was not far from where Edgar Allan Poe lived during his most productive years, cranking out macabre fictions like "The Murders of the Rue Morgue" during an earlier crime wave.

Today the few blocks around Lynch's first Philadelphia home still have the feel of a no-man's-land, but the factories have long ceased operation, and as with many former industrial pockets of American cities, there are signs of renewal and a few scattered residential developments. The square-mile area, with its brick and concrete behemoths and sprinkling of Gothic and art deco structures, was added to the National Register of Historic Places in 2010 as the Callowhill Industrial Historic District. Lynch's old row house and Pop's Diner are long gone—a U-Haul parking lot occupies the corner—and the building that was the morgue now houses an annex of the Roman Catholic high school. The combination of cheap rents, large spaces, and perhaps even the Lynch legend has attracted arts organizations to the area. While Realtors optimistically bill the neighborhood as the "Loft District," some locals, in honor of its most famous former resident, call it the Eraserhood.

5

Head Movie

THE SETTING OF *Eraserhead* is never named but there is no mistaking this infernal wasteland for anywhere but Philadelphia — or rather, the Philadelphia of Lynch's mind. He has jokingly called the film "the real *Philadelphia Story*," and even though he made it after moving to Los Angeles, shooting in that city's own depopulated downtown and on painstakingly fabricated sets, *Eraserhead* bears the imprint of Lynch's time in Philadelphia, as a young artist on the cusp of adulthood. In fact, it may be the closest this very personal though rarely autobiographical filmmaker has ever come to a self-portrait.

The hapless hero of *Eraserhead,* Henry, with his furrowed brow and electroshock pompadour, is the first of Lynch's many anxious protagonists. Henry's generalized bewilderment becomes more specific with the distressing news that his estranged girlfriend, Mary, has given birth to . . . something: "They're still not sure it *is* a baby!" she wails. As their offspring turns out to be a howling, pustulant monster, *Eraserhead* is commonly interpreted as a film about fear of fatherhood or of sex, a parable of reproductive dread. It has also become customary to bolster such readings by pointing out that Lynch became a father at age twenty-two, to a daughter who was born with club feet. There are other correspondences that cement Henry as the original Lynchian alter ego, starting with his incongruous formal attire:

He wears a suit and tie, with white socks and a pocket protector, even while claiming to be "on vacation" from his printing job at "LaPelle's factory." Lynch worked for a time as a printer and engraver for a Philadelphia painter and gallerist named Rodger LaPelle. Mary and her parents live in a house with the number 2416; Lynch's last Philadelphia residence, the three-story corner row house that he and Peggy bought for $3,500, was at 2416 Poplar Street.

Although steeped in the rot and grime of postindustrial Philadelphia, *Eraserhead* is hardly a work of urban realism. Lynch's assertion that the film "came out of the air in Philadelphia," as he told K. George Godwin in a 1981 interview, is well put. *Eraserhead* is a distillation of atmosphere, an expressionist exaggeration of the hostile environment that both terrified and thrilled Lynch. His first Philadelphia home, several blocks north of the PAFA, was in a district of warehouses and light industry that emptied out after the workday. Lynch, keeping night-owl hours, would often walk the dark, narrow streets by himself, under the elevated train tracks of the Reading Viaduct. Most of the exterior scenes in *Eraserhead* find Henry making his way through vacant lots and past derelict buildings, navigating piles of rubble and tangles of pipes, startled by mysterious clouds of vented steam and an offscreen chorus of barks. (Lynch recalls that the dogs at Pop's Diner next door were weird-looking creatures, small with distended bellies "like water balloons.") Despite its real-world analogues, Lynch's Philadelphia story is above all a film of interior states. Its droning soundscape reinforces the impression of a literal head movie, one that might be taking place within someone's pressurized, traumatized skull. Even in his room, Henry cannot escape the shrieking wind or the rumble of nearby factories; his radiator emits a constant, taunting hiss. *Eraserhead,* one might say, is less a depiction of Philly than an expression of how the city got under Lynch's skin.

For a young man who had known only small-town America (apart from a few trips to similarly overwhelming New York City), Philadelphia was "an artist's city" with "a great factory town feel." It was here that Lynch found himself "falling in love with industry and flesh," two of his most enduring subjects. Movies were one of the last great inventions of the industrial age, and Lynch's cinema has always acknowledged this kinship. "No one has gotten the power in cinema that I feel there is in industry and factory workers, this notion of fire and oil," he once said. The fixation with industry is evident throughout Lynch's work, carrying over into the soot-stained Victorian London of *The Elephant Man* and the oddly mechanical future technology of *Dune.* A sawmill is a key location in *Twin Peaks* — its smoking chimneys and sparking blades appear in the opening credits. In Lynch's long-running comic strip, *The Angriest Dog in the World,* the one panel that appears over and over, accompanied by different captions, is of a tethered dog in a fenced yard with belching smokestacks in the background. In 2006, Lynch declared his interest in establishing a movie studio in the Polish industrial city of Lódz, where he filmed part of *Inland Empire* and shot a series of photographs in abandoned factories.

The young David had come to appreciate the cruelties and wonders of organic process through observing insects and diseased trees. Philadelphia in the trough of its industrial afterlife offered the spectacle of decay on a grander scale. Here Lynch could perceive the workings of time and neglect all around him, on man-made objects and built environments. The boy who saw the world in extreme close-ups would become, as an artist, an intuitive formalist. Whether using a paintbrush or a camera, Lynch considers his subjects, human or inanimate, for their sensual or aesthetic potential, as elements of a composition; he looks at them so intently that his gaze transfigures them. "It is ugliness on one level," he said in a 1980 interview, referring to the squalid world of *Eraserhead,* "but I see it as textures and shapes, and fast areas and slow areas ..."

This Lynchian perspective, seeing the world askew if not anew, goes a long way toward explaining the discombobulating effect of *Eraserhead* on receptive first-time viewers. One of the few sui generis movies of the last few decades, it adheres to no known conventions and never settles on a tone, poised between humor and horror, combining queasy fascination and ecstatic disgust. It faintly resembles a silent comedy at times, a splatter flick at others. Describing the film's befuddled hero, Lynch said: "Henry is very sure that something is happening, but he doesn't understand it at all. He watches things very, very carefully . . . Everything is new . . . Everything should be looked at." Lynch could just as well be describing his own approach to cinema. Unlike the young turks of his generation — Lucas, Spielberg, Scorsese, Coppola, mad about movies and single-minded in their Hollywood ambitions — Lynch seemed to come from out of nowhere, from elsewhere. Self-taught and decidedly not a film buff, he arrived at cinema from an oblique angle, lacking a priori ideas about how stories should behave or what moving images can do.

The Pennsylvania Academy of the Fine Arts, the country's oldest art school, is a proud standard-bearer of the academic tradition, which placed paramount importance on representations of the human form. To this day, tucked behind the grand, ornate staircase that welcomes visitors to the academy's main galleries, are ateliers where students draw and paint from live models and a large collection of antique plaster casts. Its most famous professor, the great realist painter Thomas Eakins, in the late nineteenth century taught students to dissect corpses and cadavers to better understand human and animal anatomy; he was dismissed for removing a loincloth from a male model in a class that included female students, but many of his innovations to the curriculum endured. Through the art-world upheavals of the twentieth century, the academy made room for modernist invention without succumbing to the tides of abstraction and conceptualism. By the time Lynch enrolled in 1966, representational painting was no longer the default mode for all students. There was also a vibrant, diverse art scene in Philadelphia, and Lynch found himself within a supportive community of peers, including recent graduates and practicing faculty members who were only several years older, like Murray Dessner, James Havard, and Elizabeth Osborne. "Schools have waves, and it just happened that I hit on a really rising, giant wave," he said.

PAFA's abiding traditionalism made it a good fit for Lynch, who had taken life-drawing classes with Bushnell Keeler while in high school. His primary interest as a visual artist was — and remains — figurative. He has described his early work as "a lot of figures in quiet rooms." There is nothing quiet about what is happening within and to most of the figures, though, which inaugurate a view of the human body, carried through Lynch's movies, as a site for transformation and a zone of alienation. *Eraserhead,* a story of failed procreation within a landscape of defunct industry, links machinery and biology from the get-go, as a scarred demiurge (the credits call him the Man in the Planet) pulls a lever that propels a giant spermatozoon into the cosmos. Some of the earliest drawings and paintings that Lynch produced at the academy explored curious confluences of flesh and machine. He called them "industrial symphonies" (a term he would also apply to a musical play he staged at the Brooklyn Academy of Music in 1990), depictions of "mechanical people," "women who turned into typewriters." Most emphasized deformity and prosthesis, much as Lynch's films would, making internal organs visible and rendering biology *as* machinery, a system of orifices and tubes.

Experiments in figuration were hardly new, and Lynch, despite claiming to be unconcerned with art history at the time, was aware of at least some of his illustrious forebears. As a young married couple, he and Peggy lived in the Fairmount neighborhood just northeast of the storied museum district. Peggy had a job at the Philadelphia Museum of Art, world renowned for its extensive collection of work by Marcel Duchamp, whose many phases included one of radically fragmented portraiture. Lynch was in Philadelphia when Duchamp's remarkable final work, *Étant donnés,* completed in secrecy, was unveiled to great fanfare in 1969, a year after his death. This peephole installation affords (one viewer at a time) a glimpse of a spread-eagled female nude, holding up a gas lamp, against a bucolic scene of nature. The associations with Lynch's work are plentiful, but he does not recall seeing it as a student. It made an impression at some point, though—Duchamp's nude is the basis for a lithograph Lynch made in 2012, titled *E. D.*

The formative art encounter from Lynch's student days was a trip to New York City for a Francis Bacon exhibition at the Marlborough-Gerson Gallery, which included several pivotal works, among them his triptych inspired by T. S. Eliot's *Sweeney Agonistes.* Lynch has described Bacon as "the main guy, the number one kinda hero painter." There are obvious affinities between Bacon's and Lynch's figures, which attest to the materiality and malleability of bodies. But if in the physical drama of his work Bacon pursued what the French philosopher Gilles Deleuze called "the violence of a sensation," in Lynch's paintings and films, the horror of mutation is usually tempered by a sensual curiosity, an implicit delight in the potential for new corporeal forms. And while Bacon fixates on man's animal nature— our common status as meat—Lynch holds a more playful, surrealist view of biology, one in which man, animal, vegetable, and mineral exist on a continuum of matter.

Bacon looms large nonetheless in Lynch's early cinematic experiments. Motion was a kind of asymptotic ideal for Bacon: He modeled several works on Eadweard Muybridge's protocinematic studies of figures in action and strove to capture the sense of movement in painting. Lynch's desire to make his images move began with a moment he has recounted many times: the fabled epiphany in his painting studio when he heard a wind coming from the canvas that seemed to animate it from within. Before making an actual film, Lynch created a mixed-media contraption that involved both motion and sound. It required dropping a ball bearing down a ramp that would, through a daisy chain of switches and triggers, strike a match, light a firecracker, and cause a sculpted female figure's mouth to open, at which point a red bulb inside would light up, the firecracker would go off, and the sound of a scream would emerge. Already this pre-cinematic work hints at what would be a recurring trope in Lynch's films: a lingering focus on (usually female) mouths and parted lips.

Lynch's next hybrid piece, which he called *Six Men Getting Sick,* attempted a more elegant transition from static to moving images in the form of stop-motion animation. In keeping with his reverence for Bacon, the first action that Lynch depicted on film is a spasm, an involuntary reflex, and the work suggests nothing so much as an animated Bacon painting. Shooting two frames per second with a wind-up sixteen-millimeter camera, he produced a minute-long film loop to be projected on a resin screen with three protruding faces cast from Lynch's own head in its top-left corner, one at rest and two in apparent distress. The other three heads and the accompanying bodies appear in the hand-drawn animation, the torsos rendered as crude anatomical cross sections (except for one, an X-ray). As a siren blares, the insides of the figures fill up and their arms flail. The screen turns red and violet and is at one point engulfed in flames. The climax is a collective expulsion that all but fills the screen with "vomit" (in the form of streaked white paint); the punch line is that there is no relief, as the cycle starts again immediately.

Six Men Getting Sick cost $200, a princely sum for an art student, and Lynch might have stuck with painting were it not for a series of events that steered him further toward film. A well-off academy alumnus, Bart Wasserman, was so taken with *Six Men* that he asked Lynch to produce another "moving painting" for $1,000. But a faulty camera spool ruined all the footage, and Lynch didn't have enough money left over to create both a sculpture and the images to project on it. Wasserman agreed to accept just a film. The result was Lynch's first proper movie, *The Alphabet,* a four-minute mix of animation and live action inspired by Peggy telling David about her young niece reciting the alphabet as she tossed in her sleep. In what Lynch calls "a little nightmare about the fear connected with learning," the squiggling letters of the alphabet conspire to terrorize a painted female figure, mutating before our eyes, as well as a flesh-and-blood woman (played by Peggy), lying in an iron-framed bed. On the densely layered sound track we hear singsongy chants and distorted infant mewling (newborn Jennifer, recorded on a broken tape deck) and a voice cautioning, "Please remember you're dealing with the human form" (as a classically minded art school instructor might have, confronted with Lynch's grotesqueries). Like *Six Men,* the film ends with a violent bodily discharge: The woman spits up a Jackson Pollock–like splatter of blood on her white sheets.

Lynch continued to paint but he was hooked on filmmaking, and the Band Box, a local art house, helped broaden his cinematic tastes, introducing him to the work of Fellini, Bergman, Godard, and Tati. He heard that the newly established American Film Institute was offering production grants and, thinking little of his chances, submitted *The Alphabet* along with the script for a new project called *The Grandmother.* Lynch won a $5,000 award in part because, he later learned, the panelists had no idea how to classify his application. (He persuaded the AFI to cover the full budget of $7,118 when he showed the institute directors a rough cut.) At thirty-four minutes with a cast of actors and an actual narrative, *The Grandmother* was a big step up in scale from *The Alphabet.* In the title role, Lynch cast Dorothy McGinnis, whose daughter, Christine, was married to Rodger LaPelle, a PAFA graduate and an early champion of Lynch's work. Dorothy, whom everyone called Flash, worked alongside Lynch as a printer at LaPelle's. (The LaPelles were also Lynch's first collectors, acquiring many of his early paintings at twenty-five dollars each.)

The Grandmother enlists the hybrid organisms of Lynch's imagination to pantomime a child's-eye understanding of the facts of life. The largely animated opening sequence is an elaborate parody of the processes of procreation and reproduction: The mother and father of the story sprout from milky substances deposited in the ground; furtively groping at each other, they spawn a son, who emerges from the earth fully clad in a tuxedo. This is the first of Lynch's unhappy families: The boy wets his bed; the brutish father rubs his face in the resulting bright orange stain; the depressive mother alternates between seductively beckoning and aggressively reproving the child. Retreating from his animalistic parents, the boy finds a bag of seeds in the attic and proceeds to plant one in a mound of soil on a bed, tending to it until it becomes a tuberous growth — from which, one day, the boy "delivers" his own loving grandmother.

More than juvenilia, the transitional films that Lynch made in Philadelphia show him refining themes and ideas that would deepen over the years. Working across a range of media, he was also thinking through questions of form and content in ways that many young filmmakers never do. His first cinematic exercise, *Six Men Getting Sick,* is a clear outgrowth of his studio practice, but its closed-circuit form anticipates the temporal-loop structure that Lynch would later apply to more involved narrative films. *The Alphabet,* a product of Lynch's "preverbal" phase, points to the fraught position of text and language in his work and serves as ominous foreshadowing of the serial killer's signature in *Twin Peaks,* leaving lettered scraps of paper under the nails of his victims. *The Grandmother* is an early compendium of Lynch preoccupations, combining the biomorphic anxiety of his paintings and *Eraserhead* with the domestic horror of *Blue Velvet* and *Twin Peaks*. Replete with ambiguous behaviors and contradictory moods, the half-hour film also shows a precocious grasp of Lynchian tone, so famously hard to define and parse.

Formally, these films also establish Lynch's taste for extremes and his penchant for sonic and visual stylization. *The Grandmother* and *The Alphabet,* both in color, are notable for their stark palettes, with faces done up in white Kabuki-style makeup and much of the action set within ink-dark rooms — for both films, Lynch created the sets at home, painting entire rooms black. (For *The Grandmother,* the lab technicians, puzzled by the look of the film, heightened the color to get more realistic flesh tones, which only increased the contrast.) *The Grandmother* also marked the beginning of one of Lynch's most fruitful collaborations, with the sound designer and editor Alan Splet, who had just left his job as an accountant to join a lab for industrial films in Lynch's Philadelphia neighborhood. Lynch and Splet worked for eight weeks straight on the sound track for this wordless film, sometimes manipulating library effects but mostly creating them from scratch like foley artists in ways both primitive and ingenious. They used a golf swing for the whoosh of bedsheets being pulled back. To get a faint echo on the grandmother's eerie whistle, they recorded Lynch whistling and, in the absence of a reverb device, rerecorded it multiple times through an aluminum duct.

When Lynch had his lightning-bolt moment in his painting studio, the excitement was not just from seeing a canvas move but from *hearing* it too. The impulse to call his early paintings "symphonies" speaks to the strong synesthesia that has always guided his work. Lynch would often draw shapes for Splet to indicate sounds he wanted. As the ear in *Blue Velvet* suggests, sound is, for Lynch, the most immediate invitation into a world. Speaking of the paintings that he was creating in the late 1960s, Lynch expressed a yearning for them not simply to come to life but to become an environment that would enclose the spectator. "And you'd want the edges to disappear, and you'd want to be in there, and it would be kind of an incredible experience." *Eraserhead,* for its director and many of its viewers, would come close to realizing this impossible dream.

Lynch spent only five years in Philadelphia but it was a pivotal period and an enormously productive one. He participated in group exhibitions and even presented a solo show of fourteen paintings at Temple University in December 1968. For its press release Lynch wrote a version of the biography that he would continue using as a Hollywood director: "Lynch is a 22-year-old native of Missoula, Montana, who now lives in Philadelphia. He was an Eagle Scout as a boy." Philadelphia and the PAFA provided inspiration and a support network, but for Lynch, ever wary of pedagogy, attending classes got in the way of producing work, and he completed only three semesters. The letter he wrote to the school announcing his intention to withdraw is unmistakably Lynchian in its dark-comic inclusion of graphic medical details: "I just don't have enough money these days and my doctor says I'm allergic to oil paint. I am developing an ulcer and pin-worms on top of my spasms of the intestines." The letter is dated August 4, 1967, just a few months after he made *Six Men Getting Sick,* but already, the postscript makes clear that he had found his calling: "I am seriously making films instead."

On the strength of *The Grandmother,* which won prizes at several U.S. film festivals and screened at the prestigious festival for short films in Oberhausen, Germany, Lynch applied to the AFI's brand-new Center for Advanced Film Studies. He was accepted as a fellow in the center's second year; the officials at the AFI were so impressed with the sound work on *The Grand-*

mother that they also invited Splet to head their sound department. In August 1970, David, Peggy, and Jennifer moved to Los Angeles, joined by Splet, who accepted the job offer, and Fisk, who wanted to get into movies.

The institute's dean, Frank Daniel, a recent émigré who came from FAMU, the respected Czechoslovak film school in Prague, was an important mentor who taught classes on film analysis and script structure. But as at the PAFA, Lynch found the AFI more valuable for the community than for the curriculum. He spent much of his first year revising a script called *Gardenback,* which combines elements of *The Grandmother* and *Eraserhead.* He had a catchy spiel for it: "When you look at a girl, something crosses from her to you. And in this story, that something is an insect." This would be a tale of adultery and guilt — the insect would grow in the man's attic, as the title character of *The Grandmother* did. Not coincidentally, perhaps, it was around this time that Lynch first read Kafka's *The Metamorphosis.* The cinematographer Caleb Deschanel, also an AFI fellow, loved the script and introduced Lynch to producers at Twentieth Century Fox, who were looking to invest in genre films. This marked Lynch's first dispiriting encounter with potential moneymen (there would be many more). The attempt to stretch the forty-five-page *Gardenback* script to feature length — in effect, to normalize it — was foredoomed. "I couldn't think in a regular enough way, with regular dialogue, to make it work for them," Lynch said. "A lot of people tried to help me, but the bits that I liked started floating further apart and in between was the stuff I didn't like."

When *Gardenback* fizzled, Lynch turned his attention to *Eraserhead,* his Philadelphia story. The AFI approved the project assuming that his twenty-one-page script would be a short film and that it would be completed in a matter of weeks. It ended up as a feature — nearly six years later. The long gestation of *Eraserhead* is a much mythologized chapter of independent film lore. A wholly improbable labor of love, indeed an acme of DIY monomania, it was made under circumstances that are hard to imagine any producer or film school today sanctioning. The AFI at the time had its headquarters at Greystone Mansion, which sits within a sprawling landscaped estate in Beverly Hills that used to belong to the oil tycoon Edward Doheny. (The house has since been used for many film shoots, including Paul Thomas Anderson's *There Will Be Blood*.) Lynch was given permission to shoot in the outbuildings at the far end of the property: a cluster of stables, garages, and servants' quarters that he turned into a makeshift studio. The Los Angeles parks department used part of the space as storage and needed access during the day, so they had to shoot at night, which suited Lynch's habits as well as the needs of his almost entirely nocturnal film.

The professional relationships that Lynch forged on *Eraserhead* would last for many years. In the lead role he cast Jack Nance, who had done theater in San Francisco and just moved to L.A. in search of movie roles. Their first meeting was rocky — Nance was wary of getting involved in a student art film — but the two men bonded in the parking lot when Nance made an admiring remark about a homemade wooden roof rack affixed to a nearby Volkswagen, which turned out to be Lynch's. Nance would appear in almost every Lynch film until his death in 1996. Nance's then wife, Catherine Coulson, took on multiple tasks, from assisting with camera lighting and set decoration to feeding the crew, often bringing leftovers from her waitressing job. Coulson's iconic Log Lady role in *Twin Peaks* originates from a running joke from the *Eraserhead* days: Lynch claimed he would create a TV show for her called *I'll Test My Log with Every Branch of Knowledge*. The cinematographer Herb Cardwell joined Lynch from Philadelphia and shot for several months before having to look for properly paid work. His replacement, Frederick Elmes, another AFI fellow, would go on to an illustrious career working with Jim Jarmusch, Ang Lee, and others; he also shot *Blue Velvet* and *Wild at Heart* for Lynch. Friends and family would drop in to help, including Lynch's brother, John, living in Los Angeles at the time, and Jack Fisk, newly married to Sissy Spacek, the star of *Badlands* (1973), the acclaimed debut by another AFI graduate, Terrence Malick, which Fisk art-directed. Fisk and Spacek (who would star in Lynch's *The Straight Story*) contributed funds toward the completion of *Eraserhead,* and Fisk was also enlisted to play the Man in the Planet, buried under disfiguring makeup.

Eraserhead is an exemplar of ingenuity born of poverty. Lynch and his crew salvaged set dressing from swap meets and wardrobes from Goodwill. Scenery flats and even some film stock came from the Dumpsters of movie studios. Shooting began on May 29, 1972, with Henry's traumatic visit to his prospective in-laws, the Xes. The scene in which Henry squirms on a sofa as the impassive Mrs. X grills him was completed in a single take. But there was no way to keep up this pace with a minuscule crew and curtailed work hours — not to mention the sheer volume of stuff that had to be constructed. Filmmaking is, for Lynch, first and foremost an exercise in world building. Nowhere has this been more literally borne out than in *Eraserhead.* Almost every scene features some fastidiously handcrafted object or lovingly textured surface: the planet looming behind Henry's head in the opening shot, the twig sprouting from a hillock of earth by his bedside, the wiggling "man-made chickens" that Mr. X serves for dinner, Henry's lopped-off head when he dreams of being decapitated, the various worm and spermatozoon-like organisms, and, of course, the moist, gauze-swaddled, pointy-headed baby itself, which Nance christened Spike, and whose origins remain a closely guarded secret to this day. Even Henry's mushroom-cloud hairdo was a kind of living sculpture that, to Nance's annoyance, had to be maintained for several years.

For Lynch, comfortable in carpentry workshops and artist studios, this artisanal method was optimal. It allowed him complete control over the world of the film, as a painter would have over his canvas. Elmes joined the *Eraserhead* crew after a stint as camera assistant with John Cassavetes, the institute's filmmaker in residence, who populated the crew on *A Woman Under the Influence* with AFI students. After the freewheeling energy and willful chaos of Cassavetes's set, the neurotic attention to detail in the self-contained Lynch universe took some getting used to. Elmes told me that on one of his first days, he moved a prop a few inches to align a shot he was framing, only for another crew member to tell him, "We don't move props here."

The obvious problem with building almost everything in a movie is that it can take an eternity. Often the shoot would stop while elaborate props were completed or sets dismantled and rebuilt, sometimes in the same spot. One corner of the AFI stables served as the pencil factory in Henry's dream, the factory's front office, and the lobby of Henry's building. When the AFI grant ran out, the shoot ground to a halt in the spring of 1973. Lynch grew so frustrated during the hiatus, which stretched for more than a year, that he considered using stop-motion animation and a puppet-size Henry for the rest of the film. To pay the rent, he started delivering the *Wall Street Journal.* He eventually cobbled together some money from friends and relatives, and the AFI agreed to continue loaning its equipment. When shooting finally resumed in May 1974, Lynch kept his part-time job, taking breaks at midnight for his paper route; he studied maps and found shortcuts so he could speed through it in an hour.

All told, the shooting of *Eraserhead* spanned four years. After they were finally evicted from the AFI stables, Lynch shot most of the remaining effects sequences with an animation stand that they set up in Elmes's living room. The seamlessness of the finished film is all the more remarkable considering the piecemeal process. Not only did Lynch hold on to the highly particular mood of this interior movie for years, he rendered it sufficiently vivid for his collaborators to stick with him through countless setbacks and disruptions. Elmes recalls that the uncertainty was precisely the allure: "Part of what makes David's films unique is they're mysteries that he's trying to solve. I think we were all drawn in by not knowing exactly what was going to happen and watching him discover it."

Looked at another way, the difficult birth of *Eraserhead* was also a cozy incubation. The drawn-out shoot allowed Lynch and Elmes to experiment with stylized lighting schemes and jerry-built mechanical effects. Lynch and Splet also took their time designing the intricate, claustrophobic soundscapes so crucial to the experience of the film. They combed through audio effects libraries to find organic sounds that they altered by feeding through a console, or, as with *The Grandmother,* created them by putting household objects to strange use: To get the faint ringing that accompanies a love scene in which Henry's bed turns into a milky pool, Splet recorded himself blowing through a hose into a bottle floating in a bathtub.

After he and Peggy separated in 1974, Lynch took to sleeping on the set, often having someone padlock him in from the outside so the building would look unoccupied. Henry's room became Lynch's as well, fulfilling the filmmaker's vision of art as total immersion: He had created a world he could physically inhabit. Living with *Eraserhead* may also have brightened the film for Lynch, who discovered Transcendental Meditation during the first prolonged break. The shoot was already well under way when one of the movie's signature characters, the Lady in the Radiator, came to him as he was sketching one day. Henry's daydreams and nightmares increasingly invade the film. The most benign by far involves a blond woman in white with grotesquely swollen cheeks who materializes on a spotlit stage in his radiator, crooning an ethereal serenade: "In heaven, everything is fine / You've got your good things / and I've got mine." *Eraser-head* ends with a chain reaction of cataclysms: Henry takes a pair of scissors to the squawking baby, the baby's head swells to fill the room, and the planet explodes. "Henry goes to heaven," Lynch told the writer Gary Indiana. As Henry embraces his radiator lady, the literal and figurative darkness of the film yields to a blinding white light. This is one version of a Lynchian conclusion: A happy ending that may not be one.

Midway through the production of *Eraserhead,* Lynch edited together some footage to show prospective investors. He focused on the handful of sequences that were closest to finished, among them Henry's visit to the Xes, shot in part on the very first night. It is a pivotal scene, one that Lynch had written straight through in a few hours in a burst of inspiration. The first section of the movie with extended dialogue, it is also when most audiences realize they are watching a comedy of sorts. Lynch turns a staple of sitcom humor — the meet-the-parents dinner — into an ominous minefield of absurdist non sequiturs, a deadpan farce of misbehaving bodies. On the couch next to Henry, Mary suffers an epileptic fit, which Mrs. X assuages by grabbing her daughter's jaw and brushing her hair. Meanwhile a litter of puppies nurse hungrily on their mother. Mr. X rants about the woes of being a plumber ("People think pipes grow in their homes!"), standing before an enormous duct that could have sprung from the ground. In the kitchen Mrs. X tosses the salad with the help of catatonic Grandma X's lifeless limbs. When Henry cuts into the squab-like creature that Mr. X has roasted for dinner, viscous blood spills from its cavity and its thighs wag up and down, sending Mrs. X into a drooling erotic trance. Then comes the bombshell, "there's a baby," at which point Henry gets a nosebleed.

Terrence Malick put Lynch in touch with a Hollywood producer. A few minutes into the screening of the edited footage,

the man stormed out. "People don't act like that!" he yelled.
"People don't talk like that!" Hostile and uncomprehending
as it is, this spontaneous critique articulates one defining at-
tribute of the Lynchian: its skewed view of human speech and
behavior. This is often simply chalked up to a taste for eccen-
tricity, an outgrowth of Lynch's innate weirdness. But his frequently repeated remarks about his urban fears and fascina-
tions hint at another way to think about all the behavioral
eruptions and quirks in his films. In a mock pedantic attempt
to define the term "Lynchian," David Foster Wallace wrote that
"a good 65% of the people in metropolitan bus terminals between the hours of midnight and 6:00 A.M. tend to qualify as
Lynchian figures — flamboyantly unattractive, enfeebled, grotesque, freighted with a woe out of all proportion to evident
circumstances." Viewed through this lens, Lynchian behavior
has an affinity with what happens on the fringes of polite society, among those who are unable or who see no need to keep up
the facade of normalcy.

Wallace's reference to "metropolitan bus terminals" may not
be far off base; Lynch's formative exposures to public displays of
oddity or mental instability came in cities, on visits to his grandparents and, even more so, when he was in art school. His memories of Philadelphia, tinged with terror but also a kind of awe,
are linked to close brushes with violence and firsthand witnessing of the performative misery in the city's mean streets. Philadelphia had, he recalls, "the strangest characters and the darkest
nights. The people had stories etched in their faces." "I saw hor-
rible things pretty much every day."

One of Lynch's most striking descriptions of Philadelphia
conjures an atmosphere so mysteriously potent that it ruptures
the fabric of reality: "There were places there that had been allowed to decay, where there was so much fear and crime that
just for a moment there was an opening to another world."
The resonance of his own mythical sin city positions Lynch as

a more benign relation of H. P. Lovecraft, that obsessive world builder and most extreme practitioner of the American weird tale. Briefly a Brooklyn resident, Lovecraft channeled his loathing of human existence, in particular of the teeming turn-of-the-century metropolis, into delirious gothic fictions stuffed with hybrid beasts and shadowy ancient mythologies. Lynch, unlike Lovecraft, is no nihilist, but the two share a belief in terror and disgust as tools of sensory engagement, a cosmology where "so much fear" can unhinge the laws of nature, giving rise to "another world."

Hatched at great leisure and in near isolation, *Eraserhead* took its time finding an audience. "The idea of a lot of people seeing it was a total fantasy," Lynch said. The first screening at the AFI for cast, crew, and friends left the room quietly puzzled. Elmes recalls that it was "a little bumpy," with most people unsure what to think or say. The Cannes and New York Film Festivals turned it down. Lynch was by then remarried to Mary Fisk, Jack's sister. Mary convinced him to submit *Eraserhead* to Filmex, a festival in Los Angeles, the day of the deadline. It was accepted and screened in the same edition as Woody Allen's *Annie Hall*. When *Eraserhead* had its world premiere on March 19, 1977, Lynch couldn't bear to watch. His first review, in the trade publication *Variety,* was an unequivocal pan. The critic called it a "sickening bad-taste exercise," harshly adding: "The mind boggles to learn that Lynch labored on this pic for five years."

Word of the film got to Ben Barenholtz, a New York film exhibitor who helped launch the golden age of midnight movies in 1970, when he started running late-night screenings of Alejandro Jodorowsky's peyote western *El Topo* at the Elgin Theater in Chelsea. Lynch, who trimmed about twenty minutes from *Eraserhead* after the premiere, sent Barenholtz the new eighty-nine-minute edit (the version that exists to this day). Barenholtz was halfway through the screening when he called

Lynch to say he would book it. If *El Topo* was for Barenholtz a zeitgeist movie that he could market as a countercultural rite, *Eraserhead* was "a film of the future" that would need to be "nursed along."

Barenholtz opened *Eraserhead* at the Cinema Village in downtown Manhattan in the fall of 1977. By Lynch's count, there was an audience of twenty-five the first night, twenty-four the second. But people kept coming, enough for the film to hang on to its midnight slot through the following summer. It reappeared a year later a few blocks south at the Waverly Theater, where it ran for two more years, until September 1981. Another underground maestro, John Waters, who had scored his own scandalizing cult hits with *Pink Flamingos* and *Female Trouble,* became a vocal proponent of *Eraserhead* in his interviews. By the late 1970s, the film was a fixture on marquees at the NuArt in Los Angeles, the Roxie in San Francisco, the Escurial in Paris, the Scala in London.

To some of its earliest viewers, who encountered it in the dead of night like a stray transmission from another universe, *Eraserhead* must have evoked the surrealist vision of cinema as a path to *le merveilleux,* with a potential to derange the senses and confuse dream and reality. But even if it seemed to have arrived from nowhere, *Eraserhead* was in many ways a movie of its time. Less a story than an immersive environment, it has strong ties to what we now think of as "installation art," a term that emerged in the 1960s when a generation of artists began to rethink gallery spaces as containers for meaning and sites of participation. As one would expect from Lynch's background, there are other kinships with the art world, not least the fixation on body horror and abjection then ascendant in the work of Paul McCarthy, Vito Acconci, and others. The primary inspiration for *Eraserhead,* a city in the throes of decline, was a fertile subject and setting for American cinema of the 1970s, although the decade's other urban-hellhole movies — *Taxi Driver, Dog Day Afternoon,*

The French Connection, The Taking of Pelham One Two Three —
are generally pitched in a more naturalistic register.

The year of *Eraserhead,* 1977, was also year zero for punk,
and although not nearly as confrontational, the movie shares
something of the punk sensibility's visceral revulsion and willful
inarticulacy. As the cult grew, the aura of *Eraserhead* was bound
up with the anonymity of its creator: Who was this David
Lynch? The first profile, which ran in the *Soho Weekly News* in
October 1978, set the tone for many to come. The piece opens
by noting that even Mary, Lynch's wife, doesn't know what
Eraserhead is about and that Lynch, for his part, is "not telling."
"The whole film is undercurrents of sort of subconscious..."
Lynch tells the writers Stephen Saban and Sarah Longacre.
"You know, and it kind of wiggles around in there, and it's how
it strikes each person. It definitely means something to me, but I
don't want to talk about that." The most tongue-tied responses
come when Lynch is pressed on the origins of the baby. "Did
you make that thing?" Saban asks. Lynch replies: "That I... I
don't... I... Stephen, I don't wanna, uh... talk about that."
He adds: "If I say, I'll really feel bad." In a token concession
to interpretation, Lynch allows that Henry may be repressing
something: "He's trying to maintain, and there are problems."
"Everybody has a subconscious and they put a lid on it. There's
things in there."

Even in its title, *Eraserhead* encourages psychoanalytic readings. Is the head's eraser the superego? Is the baby a phallic symbol and is its climactic mutilation, not to mention the dream of
decapitation, an expression of castration anxiety? But the film is
ultimately less remarkable for the content than for the form of
its protagonist's inner life, less for the "things in there" than for
how it gets under that lid. *Eraserhead* opens with a slow camera move through space and toward the planet, getting closer
and closer until we are right up against its creviced surfaces. No
wonder the film exerts a vortex-like pull. Its entire trajectory is

inward, which corresponds perhaps to an agoraphobic idea of comfort. The inhospitable outside world bears down on Henry even in his room, and he finally finds solace within the warm enclosure of his radiator. "With *Eraserhead* I stayed real close to my original idea," Lynch said, "to the point that there are scenes in the movie that feel like they're more inside my head than they are on the screen." *Eraserhead* is a triumph of interiority, a masterpiece Lynch made by retreating into his own head. The next challenge, as he was soon to learn, would be how to get out.

6

Inner and Outer Space

WHAT DOES THE creator of an unrepeatable labor of love like *Eraserhead* do for an encore? Perhaps because no obvious answer presented itself, David Lynch built sheds.

As *Eraserhead* acquired a life of its own, Hollywood took notice. Agents called; a few meetings transpired. Lynch shopped around a screenplay, *Ronnie Rocket,* from an idea he'd cooked up a decade earlier on his first trip to Europe. Subtitled *The Absurd Mystery of the Strange Forces of Existence,* the movie would revolve around electricity, a primal force in *Eraserhead,* with its sparking bulbs and humming power stations, and in many subsequent Lynch films, where electrical disturbance often signals a short circuit in the wiring of reality. The title character is a midget, resurrected via electricity (like Frankenstein's monster), who becomes a rock star. Perhaps because Lynch was fond of describing it as a film about "a three-foot tall guy with red hair and physical problems, and about 60-cycle alternating current electricity," none of the pitch meetings went anywhere.

Lynch kept busy, as he always has in fallow periods. He and Mary were renting a house with a yard, and he started scavenging wood from his paper route, which he kept after finishing *Eraserhead.* He built obsessively, constructing a garage, a painting studio, sheds for storage. It was tactile, satisfying work — a more intimate and utilitarian form of world building. Asked once about his love of sheds, Lynch said, "They can be used for storage, and they can be used for little places to be."

The call that snapped Lynch out of his shed-building reverie came from a young Hollywood producer, Stuart Cornfeld, who had seen *Eraserhead* at its first midnight showing at the NuArt. The films that would consume Lynch for the next seven years — *The Elephant Man* and *Dune* — are mind-boggling leaps in scale from *Eraserhead*. They occupy a curious place in his corpus, symbolizing a path not taken. Neither is a project he initiated. Both harken back to the last gasp of a braver, stranger era in American studio filmmaking, when someone with no track record could be trusted with big budgets. This was also a time when a conventional Hollywood path was still within Lynch's grasp and, indeed — as a thirtysomething family man, now with two children (he and Mary had a son, Austin, in 1982) — was something to strive for.

In critical studies of Lynch, *The Elephant Man* and *Dune* are often sidelined, deemed less authentic and dismissed as works for hire. If discussed at all, they are scrutinized for authorial traces, through the lens of what the French critics of the 1950s called *la politique des auteurs,* a means of reading films that asserts individual artistry within the industrial processes of cinema. Because of their marginal status, both films have seen compensatory attempts at recuperation, in particular the once maligned *Dune,* now a cause for some partisans. (The philosopher-provocateur Slavoj Žižek deems it Lynch's best work — very much a minority opinion.) Both shaped the mutual wariness that to this day defines Lynch's relationship to the mainstream. One was a permission slip, the other a red flag.

Freak-show exhibit turned medical specimen Joseph Merrick was born in 1862 with extravagant physical deformities that made him an object of repulsion and fascination all his short life. His biography is often refracted through the perspective of the London surgeon Frederick Treves, who in the popular recounting rescued Merrick from sideshow exploitation and turned him into a drawing-room curiosity for Victorian high society. The story of John Merrick — as he's called in Treves's book and many subsequent accounts — has the quality of fable, revolving as it does around a gentle outcast who brings out the best and worst of humanity. Before Hollywood got to him, Merrick had already been the subject of several books, including one by the anthropologist Ashley Montagu (subtitled *A Study in Human Dignity*), and a Broadway play that at one point starred David Bowie. When Cornfeld presented him with a script, Lynch had never heard of the Elephant Man, but the title alone was for him wildly evocative.

The next step was for Cornfeld and the producer Jonathan Sanger, who had optioned the script, to convince the primary backer, the comedian and filmmaker Mel Brooks, that Lynch was the right director. Brooks's willingness to gamble on Lynch was a tremendous leap of faith. *Eraserhead,* no one's idea of a calling-card movie, cost about $20,000; *The Elephant Man* was produced at Paramount on a budget of $5 million. Lynch fully expected to be dropped from the project when Brooks saw *Eraserhead.* But Brooks could not have been more enthusiastic — he reached for superlatives, comparing it to Beckett and Ionesco — although the clean-cut, conservative-looking Lynch did not match his mental picture of the man who had made *Eraserhead.* "I expected to meet a grotesque," Brooks said, "a fat little German with fat stains running down his chin and just eating pork."

Lynch worked with the writers Eric Bergren and Christopher De Vore to revise their screenplay and to bring it subtly in line with his interests. As he would do in many later films, he set up a contrast between two opposing realms: Merrick's elevation into bourgeois society by day and his continued abuse by night at the hands of a hospital porter who turns him back into a sideshow attraction. In the alien environment of Victorian England, Lynch gravitated to familiar obsessions. The world of *The Elephant Man* is one of industry and flesh. Operating on a gruesome-looking casualty of a factory injury, Treves refers to the "abominable" machines of the industrial revolution — "You cannot reason with them" — suggesting a connection to the malfunctioning apparatus that is Merrick's body, which also has a mind of its own. Describing the Elephant Man's protuberant growths, Lynch said: "They were like slow explosions. And they started erupting from the bone."

In his first stab at a commercial movie, Lynch proves a deft manipulator of audience expectations and emotions. When Treves first encounters Merrick, Lynch shows us only the doctor's distressed face, tears streaming down his cheeks. For a full half hour, the Elephant Man remains hidden from view, behind a sack mask, in shadow and silhouette, to the point where viewers cannot help being aware of their own voyeuristic dread and desire. We finally see the full extent of his facial disfigurement through the eyes of a screaming nurse; the power of the moment lies more in his reaction than hers, in his horror at his own capacity to disgust. *The Elephant Man* is an unusual monster movie, one in which, as the French critic Serge Daney put it, "it is the monster who is afraid." The primal Lynchian emotion of fear is even woven into the backstory: The dreamlike prologue links Merrick's condition to his pregnant mother being startled and knocked down by an elephant.

Fear also defined the experience of *The Elephant Man* for Lynch, who spent a full year in England, from preparation to shooting (mainly at Elstree Studios outside London) to editing. The abrupt transition from garage tinkerer to prestige-picture auteur brought on a performance anxiety that he found crippling. "And that's the only time I really considered suicide as a way to stop the torment," he later said. The cast was filled with Shakespearean heavyweights: Anthony Hopkins as Treves, John

Hurt as Merrick, and John Gielgud as the hospital's head doctor. There were also many veterans on the crew, including the cinematographer Freddie Francis, who made his name directing gothic thrillers for the Hammer Films studio, and the editor Anne V. Coates, who won an Oscar for her work on *Lawrence of Arabia*. Having made most of the props on *Eraserhead* by hand, Lynch insisted on creating the Elephant Man makeup himself, treating Merrick's swollen form as a piece of sculpture. But the knobby lumps and spongy bulges that Lynch fashioned with polyurethane and silicone foam kept hardening into a concrete-like matter that would have been impossible to wear. Days before the shoot began, the production called in a makeup artist, Christopher Tucker, who developed a complex system of lightweight latex prosthetics that had to be applied in sections over several hours but left Hurt relatively free to move.

Despite the terrors of the process, Lynch emerged from his first commercial movie barely having had to compromise. The material lends itself to sentimentality, but amid the strains of uplift, there remains something troubling about Merrick's sweet-natured passivity and his perverse fate as the ultimate test for the masks of Victorian decorum. A nurse tells Treves that in saving Merrick he is condemning him to being "stared at all over again." The ambiguous roles of the watcher and the watched are at the heart of so many Lynch films, their compounding tensions often spilling over in a literal performance on a stage, that most charged of Lynchian spaces. Treves discovers Merrick on display, at a freak show, and the Elephant Man's final redemption happens at the theater, where he watches a Puss in Boots pantomime, sitting in a balcony box for all to see.

Some have pointed to the autobiographical dimension of *The Elephant Man,* a film about an outcast's entry into bourgeois society that marked Lynch's own ascension to respectability. When it opened in October 1980, many in the film world had never heard of Lynch; some reviewers assumed he was British. A *New York Times* piece on John Hurt before the film's release made no mention of the director; the *Times* reviewer acknowledged that he had never seen *Eraserhead*. With the notable exception of Roger Ebert, who would continue to nurse a deep antipathy toward much of Lynch's work, the major critics loved *The Elephant Man*. Pauline Kael, who had recommended the script during her stint as a consultant for Paramount, was effusive in her praise: "You're seeing something new—subconscious material stirring within the format of a conventional narrative." The film grossed five times its budget at the U.S. box office and was an especially big hit in Japan and France, where Lynch would find his most loyal fans. He could not have asked for a more auspicious commercial debut: a popular and critical success that left room for his distinctive sensibility and gained the industry stamp of approval in the form of eight Academy Award nominations.

The Elephant Man was shut out at the Oscars—Robert Redford's directing debut *Ordinary People* swept the major awards that year—but it opened doors for Lynch. He tried to get *Ronnie Rocket* off the ground again, this time with Francis Ford Coppola's American Zoetrope studio, but Coppola had to scale back his production efforts after the devastating failure of his 1982 musical *One from the Heart*. George Lucas asked if Lynch would direct the third installment of the Star Wars series, *Return of the Jedi*. Instead he opted to launch his own blockbuster franchise by filming one of the elusive grails of science fiction, Frank Herbert's *Dune*.

Like Lynch, Herbert was a Pacific Northwesterner. He came up with the idea for *Dune* while researching a magazine story about the environmental effects of the shifting sand dunes on the Oregon coast. Published in 1965, *Dune* is set some twenty thousand years in the future, largely on the desert planet Arrakis, the lone source of the most valuable natural resource in the universe, a narcotic, life-giving spice known as melange. Detailing the messianic wars that erupt over this precious substance, *Dune* resonated with the ecological and psychedelic concerns of the countercultural moment — and long outlived it. The universe Herbert created has been populated many times over, in sequels and spin-offs that continued to multiply after the author's death in 1986.

For years *Dune* thwarted every attempt to turn it into a big-screen space opera. The first to try was Arthur Jacobs, the producer of the *Planet of the Apes* movies, who considered making it with David Lean and Haskell Wexler. When Jacobs died, the rights were sold to the French producer Michel Seydoux, who enlisted Alejandro Jodorowsky, the cult Chilean director behind the original midnight movie, *El Topo.* The what-if mystique surrounding Jodorowsky's unmade film, which he promised would trigger hallucinations without drugs, has grown over the years and was further cemented in the 2013 documentary *Jodorowsky's Dune.* Its reputation rests largely on the motley troupe of collaborators the director had somehow assembled: a cast including Orson Welles, Salvador Dalí, and Mick Jagger; designs by the Swiss surrealist artist H. R. Giger and the French cartoonist Jean "Moebius" Giraud; and Pink Floyd for the sound track.

After that production unsurprisingly collapsed — Jodorowsky had envisioned Herbert's five-hundred-page novel as a twelve-hour film — the rights landed with the Italian mogul Dino De Laurentiis, whose flamboyant, up-and-down career straddled art and pulp, spanning the birth of Italian neorealism to the rise of the star-studded international coproduction. De Laurentiis paired Ridley Scott with *Dune,* but Scott, working with the writer Rudy Wurlitzer (*Two-Lane Blacktop*), failed to produce a workable screenplay. Dino's twentysomething daughter, Raffaella, who was being groomed for the family business, proposed Lynch based on *The Elephant Man,* which had moved her to tears. The De Laurentiises also watched *Eraser-head,* which Dino hated and which alerted them to keep an eye on their new hire's audience-alienating side.

As with *The Elephant Man,* Lynch had no idea what he was being offered. "*June?*" he famously said when he got the call. Once he read Herbert's opus, the appeal was obvious. Here was an opportunity to construct not one but multiple worlds — four planets! — each with its own moods and textures. At the time Herbert had already published four *Dune* novels, with a fifth on the way. A *Dune* movie, and a possible series, promised job security and the opportunity to tell a continuing story, to immerse oneself in a fabricated world (as Lynch would later do with *Twin Peaks*). Herbert's prose, abounding with gibberish neologisms (Kwisatz Haderach, Bene Gesserit, Thufir Hawat), matched Lynch's sense of language as a sound effect. The rampant doublings — people and planets often have more than one name — suited his taste for duality. *Dune* even had a Lynchian catchphrase: "The sleeper must awaken," a decree from the messiah hero's father that could apply to any number of Lynch protagonists, drifting through alternate realities in varying degrees of consciousness.

It took Lynch a year and a half and seven drafts to arrive at a 135-page script. In transforming *Dune* into a filmable screenplay, he simplified its plot convolutions and muffled its metaphorical implications. Lynch, as a meditator, might have been expected to share Herbert's interest in Zen Buddhist philosophy, but the book's spiritual overtones, along with its geopolitical resonances in relation to the Cold War and the fight for oil, were largely lost in the onslaught of data and exposition. "I'm not really getting into the religious thing in *Dune,*" Lynch said in an interview at the time. "It was vague to me in the book. I do have rites and ceremonies and traditions, but this isn't really a religious picture."

Location scouts were dispatched to the Sahara, Australia,

and India, but the producers finally settled on Mexico, where Churubusco Studios in Mexico City had ample soundstages available for a long stretch of time at comparatively low costs and was close to desert locations and a ready supply of local wood and leather craftsmen. The cast was a polyglot hodgepodge typical of an international coproduction: the German actor Jürgen Prochnow as the ruling duke of the noble Atreides clan and the British actress Francesca Annis as his concubine, with all manner of luminaries — including Sting, Max von Sydow, Patrick Stewart, and Silvana Mangano (Dino's wife and Raffaella's mother) — putting in cameo appearances. For the young messiah Paul Atreides, an unknown was needed. From more than one hundred screen tests, Lynch picked a Seattle theater actor with no film experience, Kyle MacLachlan, who looked like a younger, fresher-faced Lynch and happened to be a *Dune* obsessive.

Lynch and Raffaella De Laurentiis, who was overseeing the shoot, spent a year and a half in Mexico from pre- to postproduction. The scale of *The Elephant Man* had come as a shock to Lynch. *Dune* was a behemoth of another order, comparable in magnitude to the sword-and-sandal epics of yore: forty speaking parts, more than a thousand crew members, and twenty thousand extras. Still, Lynch was less anxious this time, having passed his first Hollywood test, and the stresses were mitigated by the excitement of being on what he called "the biggest train set in the world," echoing Orson Welles's famous description of the RKO studio lot. The production filled the eight massive soundstages at Churubusco twice over, constructing about eighty distinct sets.

Lynch's *Dune* is above all a feat of design. Herbert envisioned a post-technological future, centuries after humans had overthrown "thinking machines" in a revolutionary jihad. Lynch and the De Laurentiises appreciated the novelty of a science-fiction movie that avoided the crutch of high-tech gadgetry. Their research trips were not to NASA labs but to the architectural wonders of Venice and Florence. Even at its most narratively leaden, *Dune* is something to behold visually: a riot of clashing medieval-futurist styles; "steampunk" before the term was coined. Lynch told the production designer Anthony Masters, who had worked on *2001: A Space Odyssey,* that *Dune* should not look futuristic. "We went to the past," Masters said, "to a 1950s style of over-elaborated, functionless decoration." Each setting has a distinct look. The throne room of Kaitain, where the Emperor of the Known Universe sits, is a baroque explosion of gold, dripping in Moorish honeycomb patterns. On forested Caladan, the rooms of the Atreides castle are wood paneled with ornate Aztec-like carvings. Lynch's favorite planet by far was the industrial Giedi Prime, home to the leprous Harkonnens, which he visualized as a giant factory, replete with wheezing machinery, black oil slicks, and sickly green fumes.

"On these sets you don't have to put energy into ignoring the fake," von Sydow told the *New York Times.* The sets were so real, in fact, that they couldn't be dismantled. The cinematographer Freddie Francis had to light and shoot them like locations and had little room to maneuver, which may have contributed to the overall sense of theatrical stiffness. Lynch had little time to luxuriate in the worlds he had built, as the production quickly turned into a gauntlet of problem solving. Every day seemed to bring a fresh calamity, from power outages to illness. Food poisoning became so chronic that Raffaella flew in a chef and had a few hundred pounds of pasta imported from Italy, only to have the shipment impounded at Mexican customs for months.

But the De Laurentiises had showmanship in their blood, and their instinct was to spin the setbacks into publicity. They invited journalists and exhibitors to tour the set and Raffaella gave vivid interviews about the hardships of shooting in Mexico. One story, repeated in several articles, involved a team of three hundred men combing twenty-five square miles of the Samalayuca Desert on their hands and knees to clear the dunes of all living things, removing every snake and scorpion and cactus. The tone of the advance press was mostly ominous. With a budget of over $40 million, *Dune* was by then the most expensive movie ever produced at Universal. Few things get Hollywood reporters more exercised than a costly folly — like *Heaven's Gate* or *Ishtar* — that can be held up as a symbol of everything wrong with the industry and its excesses. A *New York Times* report from the set darkly noted that Lynch's and Raffaella's "good manners may be all that saves *Dune* from falling apart."

Lynch's involvement heightened the scrutiny. *Rolling Stone*'s profile began: "They put $40 million into the hands of a movie director who once took a bottle of Nair and removed all the hair from a mouse." The producers likewise emphasized the exciting incongruity of a visionary auteur tackling the impersonal form of the Hollywood blockbuster. "It would be crazy to hire David Lynch and then try to castrate him," Raffaella said. But Lynch did not have final cut; a crew member speaking anonymously to the press noted that Dino and Raffaella allowed Lynch to shoot scenes "knowing that they'd never use them." The producers were furthermore adamant that he adhere to a PG rating and a running time of 2 hours and 15 minutes.

When *Dune* opened in December 1984, a full-scale merchandising event with toys and board games, the critics were ready to pounce. "Several of the characters in *Dune* are psychic," the *New York Times* review noted, "which puts them in the unique position of being able to understand what goes on in the movie." *Dune* does not shoulder well the burden of exposition. Audiences were handed glossaries and took their seats to encounter Virginia Madsen's disembodied head in space — echoing the shot of Henry at the start of *Eraserhead* and of Merrick's mother at the end of *The Elephant Man* — spelling out the rules of the universe they were about to enter. One of the film's more eccentric methods of delivering information is to have its characters verbalize their thoughts in sotto voce monologues — Lynch's literal-minded way of getting inside their heads, combining inner and outer space.

Dune earned $30 million at the U.S. box office, to this day Lynch's highest-grossing film, but it was still a flop on a $40 million budget. Even before the movie opened, Lynch knew it was something to put behind him. The press notes for *Dune* quoted him on his next move: "I want to do movies that take place in America and that take people into worlds where they could never go. Give them a set of images and sounds they couldn't have any other way. Give them journeys into the very depths of their beings."

7

Now It's Dark

L YNCH'S FIRST THREE feature films take place in worlds that had to be created: a postapocalyptic crypto-Philadelphia, a reimagined Victorian London, a galactic empire of the future. But the fullest expression of his sensibility required a return to earth — or more specifically, to America, native soil for the volatile admixture of fear and desire that fuels his work. The only film that Lynch has described as partly autobiographical, *Blue Velvet* had been kicking around in his head since the early 1970s, and its driving impulses go even further back. The Bobby Vinton version of the title song, released in 1963, when Lynch was seventeen years old, was a starting point, as was what he called the "half-desire, half-idea" of "sneaking into a girl's room and watching her through the night." One of the film's most indelible moments — Dorothy's sudden appearance on a manicured front lawn, bruised and stark naked — came from a formative memory: David and his brother, John, seeing an unclothed woman in the street in Boise, Idaho, a startling sight that made John cry ("Because she was crazed, something bad had happened — we both knew she didn't even know where she was or that she was naked"). An urge associated with Lynch's childhood — a wish that his parents would argue — can be read into the film's signature passage: Its college-age hero, Jeffrey, cowering in the closet, watching with horror and excitement as Frank brutalizes Dorothy. Although not a period piece, *Blue Velvet* is awash in signifiers of the past: the vintage cars, dated fashions, and pop ballads all conjure the period of Lynch's youth. Jeffrey, in Lynch's words, is "an idealist" who "behaves like young people in the '50s."

For Lynch, a child of the Cold War and its bunker mentality, idealism is linked with the blinkered optimism of the 1950s, not the revolutionary fervor of the 1960s. But *Blue Velvet* is not just a parable about the uses of repression; it's also a sick joke about its impossibility. As Lynch summed it up: "You apprehend things, and when you try to see what it's all about you have to live with it." This is a coming-of-age story, in other words, and so many of its details — its overbright colors, its outsize monsters, its aghast fascination with sex — seem filtered through the still-forming psyche of a child. There is a picture-book quality to the town of Lumberton, which we discover through its bedrock institutions (police station, high school, diner, Main Street businesses like the Beaumonts' hardware store). Characters in the unfolding mystery are known by labels that could have come from a children's reader: the Well-Dressed Man, the Blue Lady, the Yellow Man. But *Blue Velvet* does more than take its cue from its hero's stunned naïveté; it instills in the audience the vertiginous sensations of discovering and moving through the adult world as a precocious and suggestible kid might.

"I'm seeing something that was always hidden," Jeffrey tells Sandy, eyes widening. Watching *Blue Velvet,* we oscillate between an overdetermined understanding of events and total incomprehension. We know that Frank is a sadist, that Dorothy is a masochist, that Jeffrey is a voyeur, fascinated by these father and mother figures both. But this diagram of desire barely begins to describe the perilous blur that the film generates between its characters' longings and perversions, between their hunger for experience and their need to feel alive. Even as it shows us things that were "always hidden," the film insinuates that some others will remain so, beyond the grasp of language or conscious thought.

Blue Velvet is an experience that leaves marks. It was a revelation for David Foster Wallace: "such a big deal" that he remembered the date he saw it, as well as the ensuing coffeehouse discussion with a group of friends in relation to their own attempts at narrative experimentation. The film was also seminal for Gregory Crewdson, the photographer known for his elaborately staged Lynchian tableaux. Crewdson has spoken of his profound identification with Jeffrey ("his quality of being there, but not there") and related the primal scene to his own memories of listening to his analyst father's sessions through the floorboards. In an essay to commemorate the film's twentieth anniversary, the Canadian director Guy Maddin, who shares with Lynch a taste for psychosexual excess and who directed Rossellini in *The Saddest Music in the World,* called *Blue Velvet* a "red-hot poker to the brain," "the last real earthquake to hit cinema." Crewdson and Wallace were both enrolled in MFA programs when they first saw *Blue Velvet,* and the film's impact on the next generation of storytellers and image makers can hardly be understated. Wallace wrote, "It brought home to us [his grad-school cohort] . . . that the very most important artistic communications took place at a level that not only wasn't intellectual but wasn't even fully conscious . . ."

Another wave of viewers had their first encounter with *Blue Velvet* when it was released on VHS in 1987, as home video was entering a period of rapid growth thanks to the plummeting prices of video players. (By then more than 50 percent of U.S. households had a VCR, up from 6 percent five years earlier.) It is not insignificant that many who came of age in the 1980s and 1990s — a sizable swath of Generation X — discovered Lynch in the intimate sanctums of their own living rooms or bedrooms, via a videotape of *Blue Velvet* or an episode of *Twin Peaks.* Even on a pan-and-scanned VHS cassette that cropped out more than a third of the widescreen image to fit a boxy television screen, *Blue Velvet* had an unnerving power. The intensity may in fact have been heightened for these unsuspecting, possibly furtive spectators, drawn to the movie's aura of taboo, not quite knowing what they were in for.

Blue Velvet plays tricks on the memory, which may be one reason time has not tamed its hallucinatory strangeness. We remember it like a dream, some details lodged forever in the mind, some fading instantly. It leaves phrases ringing in the ears, their meanings mutating with each echo: Dorothy's whiplash imperatives ("Help me!" "Hit me!" "Hold me!") and Frank's incantatory "Now it's dark." It also abounds with plot holes, unanswered questions, motivations and desires that remain opaque. Its most haunting impressions are its most abstract qualities: the ambience of rooms, the texture of night, the sensation of time speeding up or standing still. What we remember most about *Blue Velvet*, in other words, is how it makes us feel. No less than Hitchcock's *Rear Window, Blue Velvet* aligns the viewer with a voyeuristic protagonist. But the concept of complicit spectatorship, central to film theory since the 1970s, takes on shades of the uncanny here. There are moments when *Blue Velvet* seems to be giving shape to the unconscious of the characters—and maybe even of the audience. "What did you see?" Dorothy snaps. "Don't you fucking look at me," Frank barks a few minutes later. In ways we understand immediately and in ways we can only guess at, *Blue Velvet* is a film that seems to be speaking directly to us.

Blue Velvet, which would define Lynch in the popular imagination, came immediately after *Dune,* which nearly ended his career. After the failure of *Dune* put an end to any prospect of sequels, Lynch resolved to make a personal film, fully sprung from his head. He settled on *Blue Velvet,* which he had tried to develop a few years earlier at Warner Bros. Dino De Laurentiis agreed to produce it and to allow Lynch final cut if he would work with a reduced budget of $6 million and take a smaller directing fee. "Of all the films Dino was making at the moment, we were the lowest on the totem pole in terms of what we could spend and build," recalled Fred Elmes, who came on board as cinematographer. "But we probably had the most freedom."

The screenplay required some work — the earlier versions, according to Lynch, had "maybe all the unpleasantness in the film but nothing else," as he told Rodley. He revised it while listening repeatedly to Shostakovich's Symphony no. 15 in A Major, itself an ambiguous work of dramatic contrasts that plays with light and dark moods and the suggestion of innocence and its corruption. Lynch had planned to set the film in his home region of the Pacific Northwest — much of it came from memories of Spokane and Boise, after all — but transplanted it across the country to Wilmington, North Carolina, where De Laurentiis had established a new production facility. (Lynch was then dividing his time between an apartment in Los Angeles and a country house outside Charlottesville, Virginia, just a few hundred miles north of Wilmington, where his wife, Mary, and son, Austin, lived, not far from Mary's brother Jack.) Wilmington had the right combination of picket-fenced houses on leafy streets and shadowy apartment blocks in urban-industrial zones. Some of the signage and police insignias came from an actual town named Lumberton, less than a hundred miles away.

For the lead role of Jeffrey, Lynch stuck with his *Dune* discovery Kyle MacLachlan, whose career was also in need of a reset. To play the girl next door Sandy, he picked Laura Dern, daughter of the actors Bruce Dern and Diane Ladd, who had just appeared in Peter Bogdanovich's *Mask,* a heartwarming *Elephant Man*–like tale of a young man with a skull deformity. When Dennis Hopper got hold of the script, he called Lynch and told him, "I have to play Frank because I *am* Frank." Despite some nervousness over Hopper's longstanding reputation for wild behavior and substance abuse, Lynch knew it was a casting coup. "Dennis is so American — in a bent, sick way — but every American knows Dennis Hopper and every American knows Frank," he said at the time. For the damaged mystery lady Dorothy Vallens, he wanted someone exotic, possibly foreign; Helen Mirren was attached for a time but dropped out. He met Rossellini when a mutual friend introduced them at a Manhattan restaurant. Unaware of her famous bloodline or her supermodel career, Lynch remarked: "You could be Ingrid Bergman's daughter." They hit it off; he offered her the part a few days later.

For the first time since *Eraserhead,* Lynch had full creative control. While he didn't build the world of *Blue Velvet* from the ground up, he did construct from scratch the film's most important location: Dorothy's apartment, the single set they were able to erect on a soundstage. "The apartment was like a stage," Elmes recalled. "David had imagined a space where certain things happen in very definite places in the room." This locus of desire was built according to exact specifications based on the camera's and Jeffrey's sight lines, taking into account what he, and we, could or could not see at any given moment. Like so many of Lynch's domestic spaces — from the Xes' oppressive living room in *Eraserhead* to the ominous Palmer residence in *Twin Peaks* to the baroque mansions and suburban tract houses of *Inland Empire* — Dorothy's apartment appears to have been furnished, not to mention lit and photographed, to fulfill the surrealist ambition of making everyday objects strange. In his 1918 essay "On Décor," the poet Louis Aragon acknowledges the capacity of cinema to derange the ordinary: "On the screen objects that were a few moments ago sticks of furniture or books of cloakroom tickets are transformed to the point where they take on menacing or enigmatic meanings."

Lynch exploits this uncanny power with greater purpose than any other filmmaker. Dorothy's open-plan one-bedroom at the Deep River Apartments, with its phallic snake plants and mutely glowering lamps, engenders an immediate anxiety for reasons that can be hard to name. Elmes recalled that it took many camera tests to find exactly the right paint color. The walls and carpet as well as the lumpy sofa where Dorothy initiates Jeffrey into the rituals of sadomasochism are all sickly shades of maroon and mauve, bringing to mind the violent purples of some Francis Bacon paintings. It's a space that swallows its inhabitants whole, a womb-like enclosure.

After the moody, murky palette of *Dune* and the textured black and white of the first two films, not to mention the near-monochrome gloom of many of his paintings, *Blue Velvet* was a departure for Lynch in its expressive use of color. Elmes told me he thought of the opening as an homage to the intensely hued, erotically tinged works of the photographer Paul Outerbridge. To make the bookends more pronounced — the coda returns to the heightened palette of the opening sequence — the remaining daytime exterior scenes were shot on overcast days or in indirect sunlight. But after dark is when things happen in *Blue Velvet*. Night is the natural habitat of Dorothy, but it is also when the angelic Sandy first emerges, her golden halo illuminating a pitch-black frame. It is when Frank makes his grand entrances and works his dark magic, changing the very tone and tempo of the movie, as if sending it into a sleep terror from which there is no awakening. Elmes chose a slower film stock that would capture the density of darkness without dissolving into grain. Just as Lynch encouraged his sound designer Alan Splet to explore low frequencies, he urged Elmes to plunge some of his images into near-total darkness, pushing up against the threshold of visibility.

Blue Velvet was Lynch's last film with Splet, who died in 1994, and his first with the composer Angelo Badalamenti, who added new sonic dimensions to Lynch's work and sparked in him a deep and abiding interest in music. Badalamenti, who was called in to coach Rossellini through her drowsy cabaret rendition of "Blue Velvet" and ended up composing the film's lush, old Hollywood orchestral score, would become a crucial collaborator. For a scene of Jeffrey and Sandy slow-dancing at a party, Lynch wanted to use This Mortal Coil's haunting cover of Tim Buckley's "Song to the Siren" but couldn't afford the rights. The solution was to create an otherworldly ballad of his own. "Mysteries of Love," Lynch's first songwriting credit, combines his dazed poetry ("Sometimes a wind blows / and you and I / float / in love / and kiss forever / in a darkness") with an eerie, seeping melody by Badalamenti and the feathery croon of the singer Julee Cruise: ingredients that would be recombined in *Twin Peaks*. ("Song to the Siren" surfaced a decade later in *Lost Highway,* accompanying a climactic sex scene.) If the Lynchian exists as an auditory concept — if it could be said to have a signature sound, and contemporary musicians and singers like Dirty Beaches and Lana Del Rey suggest it does, more than ever — it is largely thanks to Badalamenti's contributions. In Badalamenti, Lynch found a partner who could do with music what he so often does in his movies: push clichés to their breaking point and find emotion in artifice.

Blue Velvet began with a Bobby Vinton song that Lynch didn't particularly like but that — years later — triggered a riot of associations in his head. It was in this film that Lynch first made use of pop songs for their direct access to the psyche, as repositories of buried longings that can detonate on contact in mysterious ways. Like many Americans of his generation, he recalls Elvis Presley's 1956 performance on *The Ed Sullivan Show* as formative — all the more so, in his case, for only having heard about it from an excited friend: "It was a bigger event in my head because I missed it." *Blue Velvet*'s traumatized account of a lost innocence is where we start to sense that Lynch's cinema is one of absence. This will only become more apparent in his later films, most of which circle around forgotten events and vanished people, tracing the contours of the void left behind.

Lynch's films have rarely fared well at test screenings, and *Blue Velvet* triggered some of the worst early reactions of his career. One response card read: "David Lynch should be shot." De Laurentiis was unfazed, but the negative feedback lowered expectations considerably, which may have worked to Lynch's advantage. When *Blue Velvet* opened on September 19, 1986, in fifteen American cities, some of the most influential critics were effusive in their praise. J. Hoberman proclaimed it "a film of ecstatic creepiness" and lauded its "boldly alien perspective" in the *Village Voice*. In the *Chicago Tribune,* Dave Kehr raved: "There isn't anything else quite like it, and it's pretty wonderful." The detractors were no less vociferous. Roger Ebert's one-star review in the *Chicago Sun-Times* bemoaned its "sophomoric satire and cheap shots." In the *New York Post,* Rex Reed pronounced it "one of the sickest films ever made." Pro or con, the reviews tended to make things personal, as befits a film that was unmistakably "charged with its maker's psychosexual energy," in Hoberman's words. Ebert accused Lynch of being even more sadistic than the psychopathic Frank Booth in submitting Rossellini to all manner of on-screen humiliations. In her *New York Times* rave, Janet Maslin wrote that the film confirmed Lynch's "stature as an innovator, a superb technician, and someone best not encountered in a dark alley."

Blue Velvet became an instant cult film, a lightning rod for think pieces, and as more people saw it, the reactions grew ever more polarized. The conservative journal *National Review* branded the movie pornographic, "a piece of mindless junk." The *Christian Century* named it the magazine's film of the year, praising its serious treatment of sin and evil and even invoking Saint Paul's Epistle to the Romans. Lines formed around the block in New York City and Los Angeles; there were reports of mass walkouts and refund demands. A *Newsweek* article, headlined "Black and Blue Is Beautiful?", described the clamorous scene at theaters. A man fainted at a Chicago screening; after having his pacemaker checked, he went back to catch the ending. Outside a Los Angeles cinema, two strangers got into a heated disagreement, which they decided to resolve by going back in for a second viewing. For Hopper, *Blue Velvet* was the crowning achievement of his latest comeback from Hollywood exile. While Frank Booth is remembered as one of his defining roles, he earned a Best Supporting Actor Oscar nomination for playing the town drunk in that same year's much tamer sports movie *Hoosiers.* Rossellini had by far the riskier part, as the reactions made clear. Her agents at ICM dropped her upon seeing the film; the nuns at her old school in Rome called to say they were praying for her. (After the media storm subsided, Lynch and Rossellini confirmed that they were a couple. He separated from Mary Fisk in 1987.)

"It's a strange world," the people of Lumberton keep telling one another, and the lasting impression is that it never gets less strange. So too with *Blue Velvet.* The critical enthusiasm at the time of its release — many reviewers put it on their year-end lists — propelled Lynch to a second, even less probable Academy Award nomination for directing. He lost to Oliver Stone for *Platoon,* which also won Best Picture. Yet *Blue Velvet* has weathered the passage of time better than any other Oscar nominee that year, possibly better than any Hollywood movie of its decade. The shock of the new fades by definition, but if it has hardly done so in the case of *Blue Velvet,* that may be because its tone remains forever elusive. To peruse the early reviews is to sense the emergence of the slipperiest of sensibilities, one that no one quite knew how to talk about. To encounter or revisit the film now, decades later, is to realize that we still don't.

The stiff acting and stilted dialogue inch *Blue Velvet* just past the realm of realism into a space without signposts that gets more disorienting the longer you stay in it. MacLachlan modeled some aspects of his straight-faced, bright-eyed character on his director — Jeffrey wears his shirts buttoned to the top — and he also sounds an awful lot like him, especially when he gets excited. ("There are opportunities in life for gaining knowledge and experience." "I'm in the middle of a mystery.") The difficulties of interpreting *Blue Velvet* are best illustrated in the night scene in the car opposite the church, when Jeffrey poses his pained rhetorical questions about the existence of evil and Sandy responds with her dewy, evangelical vision of the robins bringing love and light. Are they serious? Is Lynch? Some journalists asked him if the characters' exaggerated sincerity was meant to be funny. "You can't help but squirt out a laugh," he told the *Village Voice*. "These days to be cool, you don't say stuff like that out loud. It's almost more embarrassing in a certain way than Frank stuffing blue velvet up Dorothy."

Ebert's review faulted the film precisely for combining both kinds of embarrassment: encouraging laughter one minute, subjecting characters and viewers to obscene brutalities the next. The incursion of humor was taken as proof of an ironic stance, which in turn signaled subversive intent or a cynical detachment from the material. But things are never so clear-cut in the Lynchian universe, where sincerity and irony can coexist without canceling each other out. If anything his natural instinct is to combine them, nest one within the other, twist these familiar categories together until new registers of feeling materialize. In 1993, three years before he published *Infinite Jest,* David Foster Wallace wrote an essay on the deadening effects of television on literary fiction and the tyranny of "institutionalized irony," a language and a lens that had become our default mode of communication. Lynch, without exactly intending to, was already resisting this mode with *Blue Velvet*. This is a particularly tricky film not for an audience that doesn't recognize irony, but for one that can see only through irony.

Blue Velvet is a critical theorist's dream, a dark comedy of category confusion. "Hello, baby," Dorothy greets Frank, who snaps, "It's *Daddy,* you shithead." Within minutes, he's calling her "Mommy" and moaning "Baby wants to fuck." What is left to decipher when everything has been declared? An emblem of the postmodern moment, the film was also several steps ahead. It seemed to demand a new way of understanding narrative art, one that had little to do with traditional identification or protective irony or the sifting of symbols and metaphors for deeper meanings. What usually lurks on the level of subtext is here elevated to the status of text. When Jeffrey says he's "seeing something that was always hidden," he's also voicing the modus operandi of a film that is rife with signs yet impervious to decoding. *Blue Velvet* leaves the unnerving impression that it has done for us the work of analysis without so much as scratching the bright, shiny surface.

Lynch would engineer more decisive temporal ruptures in his later films, but *Blue Velvet* represents his most haunting manipulation of time in cinema, a palimpsest through which multiple eras and genres are visible. On the most obvious level, cars and interior decor, wardrobes and hairstyles all seem to have drifted in from different decades. Jeffrey's skinny tie and pierced ear, which goes unremarked, are very much of the 1980s, but Sandy and her classmates favor the long skirts of a more conservative time. Beyond such period markers, the movie also activates a host of archetypes from old Hollywood genres, slightly warped in their transposition to the present. Jeffrey on occasion resembles a film noir patsy, just as Dorothy evokes a femme fatale; Sandy, meanwhile, could have wandered out of a Sandra Dee vehicle.

The stars came with their own cultural baggage. The method actor who veered closest to madness, Hopper was a one-man history of the counterculture, born to be wild, as *Easy Rider's* signature anthem puts it. Frank seethes with the cumulative rage and mania of all the hell-raisers who preceded him, from the juvenile delinquent in *Rebel Without a Cause* to the ranting lunatic in *Apocalypse Now.* Rossellini's resemblance to her mother is impossible to miss from certain angles, even more so when she speaks in that husky alto. The sense that she is acting out scenarios that were expressly forbidden, maybe never even dreamed of, in the Hollywood heyday of Ingrid Bergman, who played her share of masochists in films like *Gaslight* and *Notorious,* lends the sex scenes a ghostly Oedipal charge. Free-floating signifiers abound, redolent of national myths and traumas. Dorothy is apparently named after the heroine of *The Wizard of Oz,* a parallel-universe urtext and a touchstone for Lynch; Hopper, as Lynch pointed out to some interviewers, was from Kansas. Dorothy lives in the bad part of town on Lincoln Street (an ominous close-up lingers on the street sign), and Frank Booth seems to be named for the sixteenth president's assassin.

But for all the mismatched period details in *Blue Velvet,* the film has a special relationship with the American midcentury, with what Lynch has called "euphoric 1950s chrome optimism." "From the '20s up to 1958, or maybe 1963, are my favorite years," Lynch has said, adding, "The '70s, to me, were about the worst! There can be things in the '80s that I love — high-tech things, New Wave things which echo the '50s." It wasn't just Lynch: The 1950s obsession was a 1980s phenomenon. *Blue Velvet* came a year after Robert Zemeckis's *Back to the Future,* the highest-grossing film of 1985, which sent teen idol Michael J. Fox, a clean-scrubbed Kyle MacLachlan type minus the dark side, via time machine three decades into the past. Having assimilated the postmodern tendency toward pastiche and the pop art trope of repurposing the relics of mass culture, the zeitgeist was especially prone to backward glances, sometimes quizzical but mostly fond and even longing. Peter Bogdanovich's *The Last Picture Show* (1971) and George Lucas's *American Graffiti* (1973), both set in prelapsarian times, anticipated the nostalgia cycle. By the 1980s, most major American directors had made their contributions. High school reunions serve as jumping-off points for Jonathan Demme's *Something Wild* (1986), bracketed by Fredric Jameson with *Blue Velvet* as a quintessential "nostalgia film," and Francis Ford Coppola's *Peggy Sue Got Married* (1986), in which a middle-aged woman winds up trapped inside her seventeen-year-old self. Steven Spielberg's science-fiction fables *Close Encounters of the Third Kind* (1977) and *E. T. the Extra-Terrestrial* (1982) fused two strains of Cold War nostalgia, combining alien fantasies with Norman Rockwell imagery.

The postwar years marked a watershed in the development of the American self-image. With the rise of mass media and consumer culture, the country's ideas of itself were being shaped and disseminated on an unprecedented scale. From the vantage point of the 1980s, the 1950s was both a cultural lodestone and a memory bank with plenty of recyclable imagery. This wave of boomer nostalgia crested under the auspices of a movie-star president who promised a return to the values of an earlier era and himself personified that era's popular entertainment. It has become critical custom to consider *Blue Velvet* as a Reaganite text. Reagan, a hologram-like president who sometimes confused Hollywood and actual history, also had his Lynchian aspects. Reviewing the 1942 drama *Kings Row,* in which Reagan had his breakthrough role, Pauline Kael could just as well have been describing *Blue Velvet:* "The typical nostalgic view of American small-town life turned inside out: instead of sweetness and health we get fear, sanctimoniousness, sadism, and insanity." In one of the ghastlier twists in *Kings Row,* a garish tale of secrets and lies in the titular town, Reagan's character loses his legs to a vindictive surgeon. The macabre one-liner he delivers upon waking, postamputation, provides the Lynchian title of the future president's 1965 autobiography: *Where's the Rest of Me?*

The year *Blue Velvet* was released, Jean Baudrillard published *America,* a postmodern update of de Tocqueville's sociological travelogue. "America is neither dream nor reality," Baudrillard wrote. "It is a hyperreality... a utopia which has behaved from the very beginning as though it were already achieved." He also called it "the only country which gives you the opportunity to be so brutally naive." At first blush the Reagan presidency and *Blue Velvet,* opening with a sequence that is the very definition of aesthetic hyperrealism, may seem to tell similar stories about America. There was a strong ideological bent to Reagan-era nostalgia, which is premised on pretending the 1960s never happened. Some have concluded that the politics of *Blue Velvet* are similarly reactionary. But the film doesn't indulge in nostalgia so much as induce the inexplicable chill of déjà vu. The return to the past goes hand in glove with the return of the repressed.

Lynch has used the phrase "neighborhood story" to describe several of his films, including *Eraserhead* and *Blue Velvet,* and even the planned sequels he wrote for *Dune,* which would have taken place in more hermetic worlds. Reagan often invoked the sentimental concept of neighborliness. He reminisced about growing up in small-town Illinois, where "every day you saw a neighbor helping neighbor." In the picture-book America of his imagination, wholesome values like patriotism were in the air: "If you didn't get these things from your family you got them from the neighborhood." In his famous "Evil Empire" speech, Reagan quoted the biblical injunction to "love thy neighbor as thyself." In *Blue Velvet* Dorothy introduces Jeffrey to Frank as "a friend... from the neighborhood." For the rest of the film, Frank calls him "neighbor," a word that becomes more absurd and menacing with each utterance. A long joyride scene culmi-

nates with Frank smearing Jeffrey's face with lipstick and warning him to stay away from Dorothy, in the process giving a terrifying new spin to what it might mean to love one's neighbor:
"Don't be a good neighbor to her. I'll send you a love letter.
Straight from my heart, fucker . . . You receive a love letter from
me, you're fucked forever." The neighborhood in *Blue Velvet* is
a variable environment, a relative space. Jeffrey finds the ear in
a wasteland "behind the neighborhood." When Sandy tells Jeffrey where Dorothy lives, she says, "That's what's scary, it's so
close." The point of this neighborhood story is that whatever
Jeffrey fears is "so close" it may already lie within him.

Like *Blue Velvet,* Reagan insisted that "there is sin and evil
in the world," at a time when the growing secularization of the
American mainstream had paved the way for the rise of a po-
litically powerful religious right. As the critic Nicholas Rombes
notes in his close reading of *Blue Velvet,* Reagan's "Evil Empire" speech — could this have been the one that struck a chord
with Lynch? — even shares some of the movie's concerns. "We
know that living in this world means dealing with what phi-
losophers would call the phenomenology of evil," Reagan said,
"or, as theologians would put it, the doctrine of sin." Jeffrey uses
plainer language: "Why are there people like Frank? Why is
there so much trouble in this world?" Lynch, who tends to depict moral forces in absolute terms, is often thought to hold a
worldview as Manichean as Reagan's. This fits the standard description of *Blue Velvet* as a kind of exposé, a film that peels away
the facade of normality to reveal a rotting underbelly, just as the
camera moves past the grass to discover the bugs beneath. But
this greatly oversimplifies the moral scheme of a film that, like
so many of Lynch's, thrives on oppositions — or, to be more precise, on the ever-shifting gaps between things and their oppo-
sites, which can widen and narrow and even disappear without
warning. "I'm not crazy. I know the difference between right
and wrong," Dorothy tells Jeffrey, sounding positively crazed.

Lynch has said that "contrast is what makes things work." The stark binaries in his films — good and evil, darkness and light, innocence and experience, reality and fantasy — are not exactly pitted against each other, but combined and recombined for their potential for disorientation, as reflections that heighten the overall hall-of-mirrors effect.

Blue Velvet could have taken an even darker turn. In one filmed scene that never made the final cut, Dorothy, clad in her blue velvet bathrobe, leads Jeffrey to her rooftop. She removes her red shoe — an obvious reference to the film version of *The Wizard of Oz* — and throws it off the building. She threatens to follow, leaning over the ledge for a few heart-stopping moments, before Jeffrey pulls her back from the brink. Dorothy's suicidal impulses are more muted in the finished film: We hear Frank ordering her to "stay alive," and she screams, "I'm falling," as she's driven off in an ambulance. *Blue Velvet* ends with order restored — Frank dead, Dorothy reunited with her son, Jeffrey and Sandy together — in an epilogue that has the suspiciously heightened feel of the prologue. The filmmaker Douglas Sirk, whom the painter David Salle once termed "the first hyper-real artist," perfected the "unhappy happy ending" in his Technicolor weepies of the 1950s. Sirk staged his studio-mandated finales for maximum dissonance, often by calling attention to their flagrant artifice.

Almost every review that mentions the manifestly fake robin that shows up at the end of *Blue Velvet* has described it as mechanical — incorrectly, as it turns out. The story of the robin is so bizarre it could have fit right into the movie. Lynch wanted a real bird, but as Elmes remembers it, the animal wrangler came up short: "The robin they brought us was molting, a ratty-looking bird. It didn't even look like a robin." Word got back to the production that a school bus full of kids in Wilmington had struck and killed a robin and that the driver had decided to have it stuffed for the school's science department. (Could this be the source of the non sequitur scene of wailing kids in a school bus in *Twin Peaks: Fire Walk with Me*?) The robin was not in fact mechanized but freshly taxidermied, dropped off at the set on its way back to school. Lynch glued the bug to its mouth and animated the bird by attaching wires that he was pulling offscreen.

Explaining the creepiness of dolls and waxworks, Freud described the uncanny as that which disturbs the boundary between the living and the dead. (Just a few scenes earlier, in a gruesome tableau in Dorothy's apartment, Detective Gordon, the man in the yellow suit, was standing upright, suspended between life and death, with a hole in his head but one last shocking spasm left in him.) Elmes recalled that from behind the camera, he told Lynch that the bird he was attempting to puppeteer looked too mechanical: "And he'd say, 'Yeah, it'll be great. You're going to love this!' Clearly that was his vision for the robin."

8

Welcome to Twin Peaks

B EFORE IT BECAME a widely scrutinized crime scene, the American small town of our dreams and nightmares, and the location of an earthly portal to an extradimensional realm, Twin Peaks was a place on a map: a charcoal sketch that laid out its imagined topography in the northeastern corner of Washington State. ("Five miles south of the Canadian border, twelve miles west of the state line," FBI special agent Dale Cooper notes to his microcassette recorder as he drives into town for the first time.) The map identifies the two snow-capped peaks that give the town its name (but are never mentioned in the series) as White Tail Mountain and Blue Pine Mountain. Running north-south between them is Route 21, also called "Lucky Hiway," where the WELCOME TO TWIN PEAKS sign greets visitors. On either side of the two-lane highway are the street grids of "the flats" and the "lower town," presumably where we will find such landmarks as the sheriff's station; Twin Peaks High School; Horne's Department Store, where the perfume counter girls are recruited for work at a bordello north of the border; the Double R Diner, with its world-class cherry pie and "damn fine coffee"; and the Roadhouse, the mood-lit biker bar with a resident torch-song chanteuse.

Even on this crude map, the town looks isolated. "In my mind this was a place surrounded by woods," Lynch told Chris Rodley in *Lynch on Lynch.* "That's important. For as long as anybody can remember, woods have been mysterious places. So they were a character in my mind." A town on the edge of the woods, where civilization abuts nature: a quintessentially Lynchian location. There is both poetry and superstition in Lynch's view of the woods, which calls to mind the *selva oscura* — the dark wood of the spiritually adrift — from the opening line of Dante's *Inferno,* and the forests of the Brothers Grimm, enchanted sites of foreboding and transformation. Above all else, though, the Lynchian forest is rooted in the American conception of wilderness. In his book *Wilderness and the American Mind* (1967), the historian Roderick Frazier Nash notes that the settlers of the New World had an instinctive understanding of wilderness as "something alien to man," which derived in part from the biblical notion of wilderness as a cursed anti-paradise: hell on earth.

The "errand into the wilderness," as the Puritan minister Samuel Danforth termed it, sent the seventeenth-century New Englanders into unknown terrain, a place to be feared and tamed, along with its indigenous inhabitants. That conquest, which turned wild country into settlements and farmland, and the influence of romanticism and transcendentalism, not least in the figure of Henry David Thoreau, would eventually make the natural environment seem less threatening. By the late nineteenth century, in response to urbanization, an opposite view was emerging: The wilderness was sacred and in need of protection from man, who became the alien intruder. The U.S. Forest Service was founded in 1905 as an agency of the Department of Agriculture to administer the nation's public forests and grasslands. Donald Lynch, David's father, was one of the many college graduates who joined the forest service in its period of rapid postwar development. In 1947, Congress passed the Forest Pest Control Act, which directed funding toward the study of tree diseases, a specialty of Donald's. To meet the demands of the building boom, national forests also became a major supplier of timber, as the forest service turned its attention to resource pro-

duction (at least until the rise of the environmental movement
in the 1960s). In the 1950s, the *Spokane Daily Chronicle* featured
several stories on tree blight and timber cutting that quote Donald, an expert on the ponderosa pine, the dominant tree species
in eastern Washington and the official state tree of Montana.
Donald's doctoral thesis, completed in 1958, examined the fac-
tors affecting tree growth between the Cascade Range and the
Rocky Mountains; its title — *Effects of Stocking on Site Measure-
ment and Yield of Second-Growth Ponderosa Pine in the Inland
Empire* — anticipates the title of a film his son would make half
a century later.

Twin Peaks luxuriates in the romance of the pristine wilderness even as it stokes the lingering fear of the primeval forest.
Lynch's hand-drawn map of Twin Peaks shows a few smaller
peaks in the vicinity — Sparkwood Mountain, Meadow Lark
Hill — and, off to the east, the wilderness of Ghostwood National Forest. These ancient woods are the stage for the towns-
folk's shadow selves, where teenage rendezvous, drug deals, and
mysterious rituals take place under cover of darkness. The forest is also home to such endangered species as the pine wea-
sel, the focal point of one of *Twin Peaks*'s least-loved subplots,
and the great horned owl, which figures throughout the series
as a watchful, ambiguous presence. ("The owls," we keep hearing, "are not what they seem.") *Twin Peaks* entered the popular
consciousness around the time that the northern spotted owl,
which nests in the old-growth forests of the Pacific Northwest,
was becoming a political symbol in a bitter fight between en-
vironmentalists and loggers. U.S. wildlife officials formally declared the spotted owl a threatened species while the show was
on the air.

Deep in Ghostwood Forest is the Owl Cave, where the
Twin Peaks police discover a Native American hieroglyph that
reveals the gateway to a mystical site called by legend the Black
Lodge. Also visible on Lynch's map are a string of small lakes,

the Pearl Lakes, to the northeast of Twin Peaks, where some residents have vacation homes, and one large one, Black Lake, directly north, on the U.S.-Canada border. The Packard Sawmill, the town's largest industrial facility, sits on the American side of Black Lake, not far from the stately, wood-paneled Great Northern Hotel, with its dramatic view of the White Tail Falls. The opening credits of *Twin Peaks* linger on these locations: the mill with its smokestacks and sparking circular saws; the white, ferociously tumbling water of the falls. It is on the pebbled shores of this lake, where industry and nature coexist, harboring both beauty and violence, that the drama of *Twin Peaks* begins, with the discovery one morning of the cold, blue, waterlogged body of seventeen-year-old homecoming queen Laura Palmer, wrapped and taped in a sheet of plastic.

A corpse washed ashore: This was the image that started it all for Lynch and *Twin Peaks* cocreator Mark Frost, but before they began to solve the murder, they drew a map. Most TV shows at the time suffered from a kind of soundstage anonymity; *Twin Peaks* had a strong, highly specific sense of place. While the pilot was shot in Washington, in and around the towns of Snoqualmie and North Bend, the remaining episodes were filmed mainly on Los Angeles studio sets and in the outdoors of Southern California (regionally inappropriate foliage creeping into the frame at times). Still, the show retained its distinctive local color thanks to a timeworn television convention: reusing over and over the same establishing shots of its iconic locations (diner, hotel, police station) and landscapes (cascading falls, rustling evergreens).

Twin Peaks became the kind of cult object that compels its fans to enter its world. To this day devotees make pilgrimages to Twede's Café in North Bend, which stood in for the Double R, and to the Salish Lodge, perched above the Snoqualmie Falls, which provided the exterior of the Great Northern. The most fanatical still maintain online shrines and resources, inspecting maps and photographs to determine filming locations (down to the exact bend in the road where the welcome sign was erected) and taking notice when actual settings — like the Palmer residence, a four-bedroom Dutch Colonial in the harbor town of Everett, Washington — show up in real estate listings. While part of the lure of Twin Peaks is the air of warm familiarity, the attention to everyday pleasures in Anytown, U.S.A., in its visual cues and details — morning fog, Douglas firs, lumberjack fashions, log cabins — the show is also unmistakably steeped in the Pacific Northwest atmosphere of Lynch's childhood. Twin Peaks would be about a hundred miles north of Spokane, where he lived from age two to eight. (The Lumberton of *Blue Velvet* was initially supposed to be in this general vicinity, before Dino De Laurentiis required the shoot to take place at his main studios in Wilmington.)

It is tempting to think of Lynch as the primary author of *Twin Peaks* — after all, this was the cultural event that ushered the notion of the Lynchian into mainstream awareness. But the contributions of Mark Frost cannot be underestimated. Frost had been a writer on the acclaimed police drama *Hill Street Blues,* one of the few shows of the 1980s to deploy continuing, multithread plots at a time when laugh-track sitcoms still dominated prime time and serial storytelling was the near-exclusive province of daytime soaps and their self-parodic cliffhangers. Lynch and Frost met through their agents at the Creative Artists Agency, which set them up for a potential collaboration, *Goddess,* a feature-film script that Frost had adapted from a biography of Marilyn Monroe. Although wary of the biopic genre, Lynch was drawn to the Monroe story. (His interest in troubled women, which begins most obviously with Dorothy in *Blue Velvet,* would become an obsession.) Lynch and Frost started writing together and completed a feature-length script, *One Saliva Bubble,* an absurdist comedy about a top secret military project that goes wrong, causing the residents of a Kansas town to assume one another's personalities; Steve Martin and Martin Short were attached to star. *Goddess* and *One Saliva Bubble* both stalled in development, and with De Laurentiis in dire financial straits, Lynch's longtime pet project, *Ronnie Rocket,* was also going nowhere.

Tony Krantz, then an agent at CAA, urged Lynch and Frost to cook up an idea for television. They pitched NBC a series called *The Lemurians,* about FBI agents battling the denizens of an Atlantis-like lost continent, which interested the network only as a TV movie. Shifting gears, Krantz, with *Blue Velvet* in mind, suggested something less fantastical, with a small-town setting. Frost envisioned "a Dickensian story about multiple lives in a contained area," he told *Entertainment Weekly.* But Krantz, son of the romance novelist Judith Krantz, had a pulpier reference point in mind: He recommended that Lynch and Frost watch *Peyton Place,* the 1957 movie about sex and secrets in a fictional New Hampshire town that was based on Grace Metalious's scandalous novel, which also spawned TV's first prime-time soap in the 1960s.

Television seemed a strange move after the provocations of *Blue Velvet.* The bureaucratic thicket of network television was surely anathema for an artist who prized control. Lynch has always been open about the medium's formal drawbacks: the inferior picture and sound quality and the rude intrusions of commercial breaks, hardly conducive for losing oneself in a story. ("It would be so absurd to have a big symphony going, and after every little movement, four different people come in and play their own jingle and sell something," he complained to *Rolling Stone* before the pilot aired.) He had also never been much of a TV buff. The Lynch household was one of the last families in Boise to get a television set and he watched only a handful of shows in his childhood, including *Perry Mason.* For a time in Philadelphia, he became hooked on soap operas through his print-shop colleague Dorothy McGinnis, who introduced him to *The Edge of Night* and *Another World,* two long-running soaps with distinctly Lynchian titles. But at the time of *Twin Peaks,* the only television show Lynch watched with any interest or regularity was the PBS home-improvement series *This Old House.*

Still, television offered him several advantages that were hard to resist. After the debacle of *Dune,* prime-time TV represented another chance to test his sensibility against the mainstream, to see if he could survive or circumvent the creative strictures of a conservative form. Television was also, as any child of the 1950s knows, the medium that shaped America's sense of self, even more than movies. Lynch told a French interviewer that he appreciated the susceptibility of the television audience: "People are in their own homes and nobody's bothering them. They're well placed for entering into a dream." Still prevalent at the time, the negative stereotype of the boob tube, with its narcotizing effect on a passive audience, only attested to its sinister powers, its ability to hit people literally where they live (at home, the "place where things can go wrong"). The television serial also allowed Lynch to experiment with immersive storytelling—in his almost childlike terms, to live in a story and to keep it alive as long as possible. He had done the same with *Eraserhead*—when he holed up in Henry's head and wallowed in his world for years—and he would do it again with *Inland Empire,* giving form, in fits and starts, to a story that had not yet fully revealed itself to him. With *Twin Peaks* Lynch and Frost could unravel a story almost in real time, as they figured it out themselves, bringing viewers along into the unknown.

To grasp the seismic effect of *Twin Peaks,* it helps to understand the landscape into which the show emerged. The TV terrain of the 1980s was a smaller, safer place. This was at least a decade before the term "showrunner" became common pop-culture parlance, before we came to associate hit shows with their creators: David Chase's *The Sopranos,* Joss Whedon's *Buffy the Vampire Slayer,* David Simon's *The Wire.* Apart from the occasional recognizable name, like Steven Bochco, the man behind *Hill Street Blues,* television was, for the average viewer, a medium without an author, or, at most, a writer's medium. There were partial exceptions — the hugely popular 1950s/1960s anthology show *Alfred Hitchcock Presents,* in which the rotund Hitchcock, by then very much a brand, served as host and occasional director, and Michael Mann's 1980s series *Miami Vice,* which introduced an MTV-derived expressionist flair to the police procedural — but film auteurs almost never dabbled in this comparatively lowly form.

This was also a time of uncertainty in the TV business, after a decade that had seen the dominance of the network oligarchy (ABC, CBS, and NBC) challenged by the rise of cable networks and home video. ABC, in third place of the three broadcast networks, was most willing — or most desperate — to take a chance. Whether or not the public responded, there would be guaranteed press interest in a show created by Lynch, a two-time Oscar nominee and a critics' favorite anew after *Blue Velvet,* and Frost, a well-regarded Emmy nominee. When they pitched the series, Lynch and Frost hadn't identified the killer — they didn't yet know who it was. Instead, they emphasized the mood and sense of place and explained that the murder mystery would recede over time, giving way to other characters and plotlines. The pilot was shot in February and March 1989 (also the time frame for the show's events), in twenty-three days, outside Seattle and in central Washington, and came in just under the $4 million budget. The network commissioned seven more episodes: less than half a season's worth. Whether or not the executives liked it, the pilot was too strange for them even to attempt creative oversight: It was "so foreign to their experience that they couldn't presume to tell us how to do it any better or any different," Frost told *Rolling Stone*.

The drumbeat of hype began in late 1989. The first article on *Twin Peaks* appeared in the September issue of *Connoisseur* magazine, headlined "The Series That Will Change TV Forever." With the premiere still months away, lengthy features followed in the *New York Times Magazine* (on David Lynch's "Dark Lens on America") and the *Los Angeles Times* (which asked, "Is TV Ready for David Lynch?"). Part of the narrative from the start was the perceived skittishness of ABC, which first scheduled the pilot for fall 1989, before moving it to early 1990, eventually settling on an April premiere. *Twin Peaks* turned out to be a short-lived phenomenon, going from pilot to finale in a mere fourteen months. But it is hard to overstate the impact of the two-hour premiere, which reached thirty-five million Americans, a third of the viewing audience, on April 8, 1990. Never before and never since has a television show compelled so many at once to ponder a defining question of the Lynchian: How are we supposed to feel about this?

As with most murder mysteries, *Twin Peaks* begins with a body. It is the sawmill foreman Pete Martell—played by Eraserhead himself, Jack Nance—who makes the gruesome find: a life-size bundle next to a massive log on the shore, a nest of wet blond hair spilling out at one end. Even in these opening minutes, the emphasis on detail and atmosphere is unusual. The first person we see is a Chinese woman—who turns out to be Josie Packard (Joan Chen), the widow who has inherited the Packard Mill—gazing at herself in the mirror, humming softly, as if in accompaniment to the still-audible theme music. As Pete steps out into the gray, muted light of a Pacific Northwest morning, we hear the sound of birdsong, train-crossing chimes, and a foghorn (which prompts Pete to murmur dreamily to himself: "A lonesome foghorn blows"). Before we learn the identity of the corpse, Lynch and Frost are already enacting tonal shifts. Pete's panicked call to the sheriff is intercepted by a receptionist who does a long, ditzy routine about which phone she's connecting him to. The sheriff's deputy, asked to take forensic photographs at the scene, starts blubbering uncontrollably — and that's only the beginning of what threatens to become a mythical river of tears.

The first half hour of the pilot introduces other key characters as they learn of Laura's death. These scenes, resting on our foreknowledge of Laura's fate, exert a morbid fascination. But the anguished reactions also tell us what she meant to others, and they establish *Twin Peaks* as a kind of ghost story, the tale of a haunting. Laura's mother, Sarah (Grace Zabriskie), grimly smoking a cigarette at the kitchen counter, calls her daughter down for breakfast, and Lynch, who directed the episode, plays this panicked moment — her realization that Laura is missing — with unsettling understatement. Sarah runs up the staircase, and we watch from a low angle as she opens the doors of the upstairs bedroom and bathroom. Light fills the dark stairwell, and the motionless camera simply stares up at an oscillating ceiling fan, a dread-inducing Lynchian object that will eventually acquire an appalling narrative significance. Sarah phones her husband, Leland (Ray Wise), who's at the Great Northern trying to close a deal with a contingent of Norwegian businessmen (another intrusion of absurdist comedy amid the unfolding tragedy). As Leland tries to reassure Sarah, the sheriff arrives, and Leland, knowing instantly what that means, goes numb and drops the phone.

Only Lynch would choose to follow this moment of agonized discovery by cutting to a close-up of the telephone, a recurring instrument of disembodiment and fear in his films, and only Lynch could absorb the bizarreness of this choice into the raw emotionality of the scene. His camera pans along the dangling phone cord down to the receiver on the floor, as Sarah's gulping sobs on the other end of the line reach a glass-shattering pitch. We witness another round-robin of grief when news reaches the high school and the camera lingers on Laura's empty chair. Intuiting what has happened before anything is said, Laura's best friend, Donna, bursts into tears, and Laura's secret boyfriend, James, lip quivering, clenches his pencil so tightly that he snaps it. The school principal, choking up, can barely get through the announcement. When we return from the commercial break, Sarah Palmer is still bawling.

Crying has always been a fundamental pleasure of moviegoing: The dark of the theater sanctions the semipublic show of what society considers a private activity. Many different types of movies — not just weepies and tearjerkers, to use two typically pejorative terms — are engineered to wring tears. Lynch himself is a crier. "Sometimes I just sit in the editing room and weep," he told Rodley. While he was making *The Straight Story,* his most conventionally sentimental film, tears would stream down his face as he looked at the monitor. He can "burst into tears" on hearing a snatch of music: Otis Redding's "I've Been Loving You Too Long" or Harry Dean Stanton's version of "Everybody's Talkin'." There is crying in every Lynch movie, beginning with the inhuman baby shrieks in *Eraserhead.* The weeping reaches baroque proportions in his later films: *Mulholland Drive,* with the "Llorando" sequence in Club Silencio, and *Inland Empire,* which is framed as a story that is being watched by a weeping woman. But never do the tears flow as profusely as in *Twin Peaks,* especially from Laura's parents, the forever keening Sarah, and Leland, given to ever more elaborate and mortifying expressions of grief. He breaks into a tortured slow-motion jitterbug, head in his hands, causing the bemused guests at the Great Northern to imitate his gestures. At Laura's funeral he collapses atop her coffin as the malfunctioning casket lift causes it to rise and fall obscenely.

Appearing on *The Phil Donahue Show,* Mark Frost addressed these extravagant displays of mourning. "Real grief isn't something that happens and ends immediately before the next commercial," he said. "There are consequences to violent crime and violent death that most television shows never deal with." Not that *Twin Peaks* exactly strives for realism. In fact, for contemporary audiences who associate screen waterworks with the wet-cheeked stars of silent movies and old Hollywood, there is something anti-realistic about its copious tears. "It's like a yawn: it transfers over," Lynch has said of all the crying fits in his movies. But to depict tears is not always to elicit them. The viewer of *Twin Peaks,* confronted with its lachrymal torrent, is less likely to succumb to empathetic weeping than to be discomfited or perhaps confused. Like so much else in Lynch's work, his tears have a paradoxical effect. They are not exactly a means of communion, a way to bind audience to character, but function more as an alienation effect — reminding us of our position as voyeurs, unnerving us with their intensity and duration, and preempting our own tears.

In a 2011 interview with the *Boston Phoenix,* Grace Zabriskie, who would take on similarly high-wire roles with Lynch again in *Wild at Heart* and *Inland Empire,* recalled watching the pilot with an audience: "People are crying — they're crying with Sarah's grief — and some people are laughing because I've just gone that little half-step too far. They got it. They're laughing, but the other ones, they didn't get it, and they're pissed off that someone would dare laugh at this terribly sad thing. Everything for me comes down to tone. One of my favorite things in the world to do is to make someone laugh and cry at the same time, and it's rare material that offers that kind of opportunity."

The crying on *Twin Peaks,* almost symphonic in its scope and range, calls to mind Nietzsche's claim: "I cannot differentiate between tears and music." If Lynch is an aesthetician of sadness, he is also one who does not shy from the ugly cry. The performers he most frequently calls upon to weep — Zabriskie, Sheryl Lee, Laura Dern — commit to the task with strident, full-throated sobs and a battery of facial convulsions and contortions. For Lynch, drawn as always to the corporeal, the act of crying—a physical expression and a physiological process—is itself a source of fascination. It is no wonder that Lynch would find tears so powerful and eloquent. Crying often takes the place of speech. A language of the body, it insists that words are not enough.

As with all soap opera towns, almost everyone harbors a secret or leads a double life in Twin Peaks. The hotel owner is sleeping with the late sawmill owner's sister and plotting a takeover from the heiress, who is having a clandestine affair with the sheriff. The diner owner is cheating on her abusive husband with her high school sweetheart, the town mechanic, while one of her employees is two-timing her own abusive husband with one of Laura Palmer's ex-boyfriends. Eccentrics are well represented: the eye-patched Nadine, obsessed with creating silent drape runners; the crackpot psychiatrist Dr. Jacoby, with his two-toned glasses and Hawaiiana-cluttered office; the Log Lady, who receives oracular messages from the wood stump cradled in her arms (ponderosa pine, naturally). And that's not even counting the characters who seem to have drifted in from alternate dimensions: the One-Armed Man; the Giant; the dancing, backward-speaking dwarf known as the Man from Another Place; and the denim-jacketed, straggly-haired, soul-snatching demonic entity BOB.

The two most important figures in the Twin Peaks cosmos—FBI special agent Dale Cooper, the outsider through whom we discover this terrain, and the dead Laura Palmer, the reason he was summoned there—meet only in dreams, or rather, in the red-draped dreamscape of the Red Room. The clean-cut, pomaded Cooper, with his nose for mystery, could be a slightly older Jeffrey Beaumont from *Blue Velvet,* looking for "something that was always hidden." A connoisseur of the everyday, almost comically alert to his surroundings ("I've never seen so many trees in my life"), he also shares Lynch's Boy Scout enthusiasm, sweet tooth, and openness to Eastern mysticism. Laura haunts the show from the moment the plastic shroud is peeled from her face, as delicately as a bridal veil. She appears repeatedly, beaming under a tiara, in her homecoming-queen headshot, which is on proud display in the high school's trophy case and the Palmer living room. This wholesome picture of Laura, which also accompanies the end credits of the initial episodes, contradicts the one that gradually emerges of her as drug addled, promiscuous, manipulative, damaged, fearful, and self-destructive. In this pivotal role, Lynch had cast Sheryl Lee, a twenty-two-year-old actress from Seattle, off a headshot. For the pilot her sole assignment was to play dead, except for one scene in which she appears in a video recording, dancing with Donna and flirting with the camera. Lynch was so struck by Lee's radiance as the living, breathing Laura that he wheeled out the old soap-opera trope and wrote her into the show as Laura's look-alike cousin, Madeleine, only to subject her to a similar fate.

Lynch told *Time* that he hoped *Twin Peaks* would "cast a spell." It certainly did on the press, which couldn't stop writing about it. Critics reveled in the incongruity of Lynch on prime time ("This all-American surrealist takes to television like a parasite to an especially nourishing host," declared the *New Yorker*). While soap opera magazines profiled the cast members, the critic John Leonard, in a *New York* magazine cover story, described the show as an obsession of the intelligentsia, dropping names from Antonioni to Wittgenstein. "Television, the talking furniture we look to as a cure for loneliness, is not expected to surprise," Leonard wrote.

Twin Peaks didn't break the rules of dramatic television so much as subtly derange them. It slowed down the narrative tempo and destabilized the emotional temperature. It expanded the vocabulary of the small screen, departing from the norm of inconspicuous medium shots with arresting compositions and a rich, subtly stylized color scheme (Lynch is said to have banned blue props). But its novelty was only one reason it became a phenomenon so quickly, and perhaps not the main one. From the title's jokey insinuation of a nurturing bosom, *Twin Peaks* privileges comfort, perhaps of the regressive variety, beginning with Angelo Badalamenti's liquid theme song, a uterine cocoon of lush synthesizer Muzak. (In a video interview for a DVD release, Badalamenti recalls that he improvised the music at his Fender Rhodes keyboard with Lynch next to him setting the scene: "OK, Angelo, we're in the dark woods now, and there's a soft wind through the sycamore trees . . .")

For all the terrible things that keep happening and the terrors lurking in the dark, life is good in Twin Peaks, as Cooper notes repeatedly, pausing to extol the crisp Cascadia air and the sweet, homey pleasures of cherry pie and jelly doughnuts. (Lynch has often referred to sugar as "granulated happiness.") Like *Blue Velvet,* the show activated a nostalgia in the boomer audience for seeming to take place simultaneously in the present day and in the 1950s. The teenage girls wear sweater sets and saddle shoes, and the bad boys seem to have sauntered right out of *Rebel Without a Cause.* "When the light is right in old neighborhoods, you get a rush from your childhood, and then a modern car drives through bringing the two things together," Lynch told *Elle* magazine. "This happened when we were shooting in the school, which was built in the '50s. Something from that era started floating around in the present and influenced many things that took place on the set."

Running within a six-week span in the spring of 1990, the first batch of *Twin Peaks* episodes ignited a full-blown media frenzy. *Rolling Stone* put "The Women of *Twin Peaks*"—Lara Flynn Boyle, Sherilyn Fenn, and Mädchen Amick—on its cover, while Sheryl Lee, dubiously draped in plastic, landed on the cover of *Esquire*'s "Women We Love" issue. *Twin Peaks* fever occasioned a *New York Times* editorial: "Is there an overbooked restaurant you've been longing to get into? Try tonight around 9." The tabloid *Star* published a loosely sourced report on sordid doings in the woods near Snoqualmie involving animal sacrifices and chainsaw duels. Kyle MacLachlan hosted an episode of *Saturday Night Live,* which included an obligatory *Twin Peaks* skit (with Mike Myers as the Man from Another Place) spoofing Agent Cooper's stubbornly bizarre methods. *Sesame Street* paid tribute with its own parody: *Twin Beaks.* The Television Critics Association voted *Twin Peaks* program of the year and it earned fourteen Emmy nominations, including five for Lynch for writing and directing (it ended up winning only for editing and costume design).

There were obsessive TV fans before *Twin Peaks* — the Trekkie devotees of *Star Trek,* most obviously — but the show introduced a new kind of fandom. *Twin Peaks* was a mass-culture text that called for communal decoding, a semiotic wonderland of clues, symbols, and red herrings. Suited equally to the scrutiny of fanzines and dissertations, it was the most recorded show on television (in the cumbersome days of VHS) and encouraged uncharacteristically close readings from TV critics in the *Los Angeles Times* and the *New York Post,* who even conducted frame-by-frame analyses of key episodes. The murder of Laura Palmer was only the first mystery and main marketing hook; the dream sequences and otherworldly forces suggested a larger underlying mythology to parse and untangle. In interviews at the time, Frost referred to the show, in the parlance of postmodernism, as "a cultural compost heap." *Twin Peaks* rewarded film-savvy viewers with references to classic Hollywood: Laura's name recalled another famous absent subject, the title character of Otto Preminger's classic noir from 1944; calling her doppelgänger Madeleine was a blatant nod to Hitchcock's *Vertigo* (1958).

Viewership fell off after the first few weeks, but many of the fans who remained — about seventeen million, half the initial number, a month into the run — were hugely invested. Long before TV recaps and live tweeting, *Twin Peaks* was an early Internet phenomenon. Back when electronic bulletin boards were still primarily the domain of academics and researchers, the discussion group alt.tv.twinpeaks averaged twenty-five thousand subscribers and one hundred to two hundred posts a week at its peak. Fans congregated after each episode in an interpretive frenzy, deciphering riddles and sharing increasingly elaborate hypotheses. In a paper on *Twin Peaks* online fandom presented at the Society for Cinema Studies Conference in 1990, the media scholar Henry Jenkins described the show as "the perfect text for this computer-based culture," one that combined "the syntagmatic complexity of a mystery with the paradigmatic plenitude of the soap."

What *Twin Peaks* fans had in common — whether theorizing on the Internet, exploring Pacific Northwest shooting locations, or, in Japan, where interest was especially intense, staging mock Laura Palmer funerals — was a desire to exist longer in its world. The producers, working with Lynch and Frost, fed the hunger by creating extratextual merchandising tie-ins that expanded its universe, including two diary-novels (from the points of view of Laura Palmer and Agent Cooper) and a travel guide to the town. But while its most loyal fans were content to linger indefinitely in Twin Peaks, many viewers were counting on the show to deliver on its promise of a solution. When it finally materialized, amid a growing chorus of complaints that it was taking audiences for a ride, the revelation that Laura Palmer was raped and murdered by her own father was not many people's idea of a satisfactory answer.

The question of what killed *Twin Peaks* is inextricably linked to that of who killed Laura Palmer. When the series identified the culprit, it also committed a kind of symbolic suicide. At least that's how the lore goes. But a closer look at the rise and fall of *Twin Peaks* suggests that it may have been doomed from the start, given the suspicion and skepticism that accompanied the hype. In a *Washington Post* piece from September 1989, half a year before the pilot aired, NBC executive Brandon Tartikoff said: "I probably would want to live in a country where something like that could work, but I suspect it will be a tough road for them." The major news stories leading up to the premiere were notable for their hyperbole but also for the constant insinuation that Lynch was not remotely ready for prime time. "Is Hollywood's reigning eccentric too weird for TV?" asked the *New York Times Magazine.* Pressed by the *Los Angeles Times* on whether he could deliver a conventional resolution to a mystery, Lynch lost his patience: "Closure. I keep hearing that word . . . As soon as a show has a sense of closure, it gives you an excuse to forget you've seen the damn thing."

For Lynch, the attraction of the serial form was precisely the freedom that it offered, even if momentary, from obligations like closure. For the network and a sizable portion of the TV audience, at a time when most shows tied up loose ends and reverted to the status quo in time for the late news, the idea that the creators of *Twin Peaks* might be making it up as they went along was cause for alarm. "It had better be able to satisfy the whodunit desires of viewers weaned on *Columbo* and *Perry Mason,*" the *Chicago Tribune* cautioned before the *Twin Peaks* pilot had even aired. At the start of the second season, with no clear answers forthcoming, the TV critic for the *Orlando Sentinel* complained: "I don't like being taken for a sucker."

Frost and Lynch have always maintained that they had identified Leland as the killer from very early on. "We knew, but we didn't even hardly whisper it when we were working," Lynch told Chris Rodley. "We tried to keep it out of our conscious mind." Lynch's account of the process implies he was working with some degree of spontaneity. The BOB character, the show's version of evil incarnate, and the Red Room, its signature alternate reality, didn't occur to him until the pilot was well under way. In the most frequently recounted *Twin Peaks* production story, Lynch has described the emergence of BOB as a happy accident. Frank Silva, a set dresser, was moving furniture around Laura's bedroom during the pilot shoot when Lynch decided on the spot to cast him. Trying to sneak past a doorway, Silva was accidentally reflected in a mirror in a later scene with Grace Zabriskie, in which Sarah, in a drugged stupor, sees a vision and sits bolt upright on the couch. Lynch decided to leave it in as the final shot of the pilot, Silva's indistinct reflection visible for barely a second in the mirror behind a screaming Sarah.

The Red Room came to Lynch fully formed when he was racking his brains for a way to resolve the pilot, which for contractual reasons needed to exist as a stand-alone movie for the European home video market. Coming out of a production facility in Los Angeles on a hot day while editing the pilot, Lynch put his hands on the roof of a car "and — *sssst!* — the Red Room appeared," he wrote in *Catching the Big Fish,* complete with its red drapes, marble statues, zigzag black-and-white floor (recalling Henry's lobby in *Eraserhead*), and mysterious denizens including the backward-speaking dwarf. The European cut ends in the Red Room and fingers BOB as the killer without connecting him to Leland. A deus ex machina to begin with, the Red Room became increasingly central. Lynch introduced it in the series proper in episode 3, which he directed, as a cryptic dream sequence in which an aged Agent Cooper meets Laura. This was also the episode that clearly signaled *Twin Peaks* was in no rush to resolve the whodunit. Cooper delivers a lecture on the history of Tibet and the plight of the Tibetan people, and using a deductive technique of "mind-body coordination," he proceeds to narrow down the list of suspects by throwing rocks at bottles. Upon waking from his Red Room dream, he phones Sheriff Truman to announce that he knows who killed Laura.

By the next morning—and the start of the next episode—he has forgotten.

Blue Velvet's wide-eyed Jeffrey was less a detective than a snoop and voyeur; many of Lynch's later films are structural puzzles that oblige the viewer to play detective. *Twin Peaks* remains perhaps the only one of his works that fits properly in the category of detective fiction, the genre Edgar Allan Poe more or less invented with "The Murders of the Rue Morgue." In some ways Cooper fits within the old tradition of the eccentric detective, with Sheriff Truman as his straight-man sidekick. But *Twin Peaks* breaks more rules of the genre than it obeys. A group of British mystery writers, including G. K. Chesterton, formed the Detection Club in the 1930s; one of its members, Ronald Knox, who was also a Catholic priest, came up with the group's "ten commandments of detective fiction." The list is somewhat tongue-in-cheek but it is striking to note just how many of the monsignor's decrees *Twin Peaks* directly contravenes: Knox prohibits "supernatural or preternatural agencies," secret passages, the use of intuition, and the presence of twins and doubles. The *Twin Peaks* approach is closer to that of Jorge Luis Borges, another adherent of Poe's who updated detective fiction for the modernist age and said that "the solution of a mystery is always less impressive than the mystery itself." For Lynch, who later said that he had planned to reveal Laura's killer only at the very end of the series, the pleasures of the detective genre are in the unfolding; the very presence of mystery suggests realms of possibility, a transformative way of looking at the world.

The dominant media narrative—even in the *SNL* skit, in which MacLachlan, in character as Cooper, bullheadedly ignores plain-as-day evidence about the killer—was that *Twin Peaks* was toying with viewers. Nervous executives at ABC summoned Lynch and Frost in for a series of meetings and strong-armed from them an assurance that the murder would be solved sooner rather than later. With great fanfare, the network took out newspaper ads in advance of the second season's seventh episode: "Finally. Saturday, November 10th. Find out who killed Laura Palmer. Really." Lynch and Frost told almost no one that Leland was the killer until they absolutely had to. The actor Ray Wise found out just before he received the script for the episode, directed by Lynch. In one of the most shockingly violent murders ever shown on network TV, Leland—possessed by the malevolent BOB—thrusts Maddy headfirst into a framed picture on the living room wall. To minimize the likelihood of leaks, an alternate version of the scene was also shot with Richard Beymer in which Benjamin Horne does the deed.

The episodes that followed the revelation were dominated by haphazard plots involving aliens (possibly a leftover strand from *The Lemurians*), Civil War reenactments, and a pre-*X-Files* David Duchovny as a transgendered FBI agent. Kyle MacLachlan, who was dating Lara Flynn Boyle, nixed a romantic subplot that would pair Agent Cooper with Sherilyn Fenn's sultry Audrey. Frost and in particular Lynch were only peripherally involved for long stretches of the second season. Frost was preparing his feature directing debut, *Storyville,* a southern gothic thriller starring James Spader. Lynch had filmed his own distinctive stab at southern gothic—his fifth feature, *Wild at Heart*—in the fall of 1989, and was tied up with its release during production of the second season as well as with a solo art exhibit at the Museum of Contemporary Art in Tokyo.

In what was widely seen as a bid to euthanize the show, ABC moved *Twin Peaks* to the television wasteland of Saturday night at the start of the second season. Ratings continued to decline, and in February 1991, the network put the show on hiatus, to the ire of die-hard fans, who formed a group called COOP (Coalition Opposed to Offing *Peaks*) and mounted a letter-writing campaign. Lynch appeared on *Late Show with David Letterman* to protest the Saturday slot—explaining that *Peaks* fans were "party people"—and encouraged viewers to write to

Bob Iger, the president of ABC's entertainment division, to keep the show on the air. ABC, which received more than ten thousand letters, agreed a few weeks later to let Lynch and Frost finish out the season in the show's original Thursday time slot, but its fate seemed obvious by then.

Lynch returned to the *Twin Peaks* set in March 1991 to direct the season finale knowing that it would likely be the very last episode. The prospect of finality didn't compel Lynch to wrap things up but to leave them even more open. Frost had collaborated on the script with two of the show's main writers, Robert Engels and Harley Peyton, but Lynch rewrote it extensively and even improvised on set. For one thing, he brought back the entire Palmer clan and the Log Lady. A scene at the diner from the pilot, in an unsettling moment of déjà vu, plays out again, word for word. The Black Lodge, much discussed in prior episodes as a purgatorial spirit world, turns out to contain Lynch's Red Room. Nearly half the episode — still perhaps the most unhinged and disturbing hour of television of all time — consists of Cooper pacing the curtained recesses of the Red Room/Black Lodge, where lights flicker, everyone talks backward, coffee turns thick as tar, and time seems to stand still. He encounters the show's supernatural forces, BOB and the Man from Another Place, and dead-eyed versions of Leland and Laura as well as his own evil doppelgänger. The two Coopers chase each other through the lodge, but only one emerges outside. *Twin Peaks* ends with Cooper, back in his hotel room, bashing his head into the bathroom mirror, maniacally laughing as he sees BOB reflected in the cracked glass. Lynch ended the series by bringing it back in line with his obsessions, wiping away hours of belabored quirkiness with an abrupt, chilling turn to the darkness within.

9

It Is Happening Again

THE YEARS BETWEEN *Blue Velvet* and *Twin Peaks* saw Lynch's emergence as a bona fide public figure, a curious turn of events for a filmmaker once associated with the midnight-movie circuit and then with one of Hollywood's most notorious flops of all time. As the romantic partner of an actress-supermodel, he was deemed automatically worthy of media attention. Celebrity photographers immortalized his relationship with Isabella Rossellini in what inevitably seemed like Lynchian poses. In one Helmut Newton portrait of the couple, equal parts tender and troubling, Rossellini, eyes closed, has her head back at an angle; the bequiffed Lynch, his facial expression only partially visible, rests his fingers on her neck, poised for a caress or something more sinister. In a more playful shot by Annie Leibovitz, which helped seal Lynch's place as America's favorite genius weirdo of the moment, Rossellini, her dress strap off her shoulder, has her arm around a semi-masked Lynch, his face almost fully obscured by a pulled-up black turtleneck.

Rossellini and Lynch lived on opposite coasts during their five years together. "I don't know what he does in Los Angeles," she told a *Vanity Fair* reporter in 1987, a year into their relationship. But Lynch visited her frequently in Manhattan and at her country home in the Long Island village of Bellport. The poised, mediagenic Rossellini helped shape Lynch's image as she discussed their collaborations in the press. She chided him for his reticence in joint interviews ("David, now you're being too enigmatic"), called him "a serene, calm, very sweet man," and also revealed that he was laughing uncontrollably while film- ing the brutal sex scene between Frank and Dorothy in *Blue Vel- vet:* "David is obsessed with obsession. He finds it irresistibly funny." In one of the most unerring thumbnail sketches anyone has offered of Lynch, she described him as "someone who has kept his life quite simple so that he doesn't have to think about it — so that he can just sit and follow his visions." Lynch broke up with Rossellini in 1991, leaving her "totally brokenhearted," she writes in her 1997 memoir, *Some of Me.* She speaks of him fondly in the book but also backs up the customary picture of a remote savant: "From the glazed expression he often had in his eyes, I could always deduce when he wasn't listening to me. I suspect he lingers in other dimensions."

The Lynch profiles from the time of *Twin Peaks* home in on quirks and oddities. Michael Ontkean, who played Sheriff Truman on the show, told a *Rolling Stone* reporter that Lynch one day reached into his pocket as they were about to roll cam- era and pulled out "the ear from *Blue Velvet.*" Lynch corrected the journalist: It wasn't the same ear. Someone had sent it to him "and I just happened to have it in my pocket." Another fre- quently repeated story had it that Lynch kept a preserved uterus on his desk. This turned out to have been a gift from Raffa- ella De Laurentiis, who had a hysterectomy and thought Lynch would appreciate the souvenir. (He was still answering ques- tions about the uterus nearly twenty years later: "It was never on my desk," he said in 2007, "it's somewhere in the house.")

When journalists weren't focusing on Lynch's supposed bi- zarreness, they were focusing on his bizarre normalcy. As if tak- ing their cue from his method, writers would poke at an ap- parently bland surface, hoping to find a perverse underside. A recurring narrative emerged: Lynch was a creature of habit who enjoyed the simple things in life, though the habits were so obsessive they verged on pathological. He told Jay Leno on *The Tonight Show* that for seven straight years he drank a chocolate milkshake in a silver goblet every day at 2:30 p.m. at Bob's Big Boy in Los Angeles. He also revealed that he tended to eat the exact same thing every day (at the time, a tuna sandwich) until he got sick of it and switched to something else. (In late 2001, when another journalist thought to check in on his diet, he had moved on to a "salad that's put in a Cuisinart so each bite tastes the same.") But cooking was strictly forbidden at home: "The smell of cooking—when you have drawings, or even writings— that smell would go all over my work. So I eat things that you don't have to light a fire for." His home in the Hollywood Hills was spartan, almost bare. This was before he started seriously designing and building his own tables, chairs, and lamps, and since he rarely came across furniture that he liked, he left the house unfurnished: "I like a real spare feel. The way the Japanese live is thrilling to me."

Blue Velvet should have opened doors for Lynch, but project after project fell apart largely because of the financial woes of his erstwhile patron Dino De Laurentiis. He kept busy in other ways. Through Rossellini, he met Leo Castelli, at the time the most powerful art dealer in the country. Castelli was impressed with Lynch's paintings. "This man knows what he's doing," he told *Vanity Fair,* adding, "I would like to know how he got to this point; he cannot be born out of the head of Zeus." Castelli bestowed on Lynch a solo show at his SoHo gallery in February 1989, to the horror of the New York art establishment ("The era of the dilettante is upon us," one reviewer sniped, deploring the paintings' "forced naivete"). In the year or so before *Twin Peaks* came on the air, Lynch acted opposite Rossellini in *Zelly and Me,* an indie drama directed by Tina Rathborne, who would direct a few *Peaks* episodes; directed a few moody perfume commercials for Calvin Klein Obsession; continued to produce weekly installments of his comic strip, *The Angriest Dog in the*

World, for the *L.A. Reader;* and staged an avant-garde musical, *Industrial Symphony No. 1,* at the Brooklyn Academy of Music, with a lumber-sawing dwarf, floating baby dolls, copious smoke and fog, Angelo Badalamenti's music from *Twin Peaks* warbled by Julee Cruise from inside a car trunk, and projected scenes featuring Laura Dern's and Nicolas Cage's characters from a film he had just shot, *Wild at Heart.*

While *Eraserhead* and *Blue Velvet* were shaped by their long incubations, it's fitting that *Wild at Heart* came together in a relative blink. The road movie is a genre built for speed. Lynch read the source novel, by the Bay Area writer Barry Gifford, when it was still in galleys. Monty Montgomery, an associate producer of *Twin Peaks* (he would go on to play the cowboy in *Mulholland Drive*), had brought Lynch the book as a project for himself to direct, with Lynch as executive producer. But when Lynch fell for Gifford's cock-eyed southern gothic noir, Montgomery stepped aside, agreeing to serve instead as producer. Lynch wrote the screenplay in six days flat. The film went into production in August 1989, two months after funding was secured, and was completed nine months later, just days before its premiere at the Cannes Film Festival; Lynch flew to France with the print stashed under his seat.

Gifford's book, which would kick off a seven-volume saga spanning some six decades in the lives of Sailor Ripley and Lula Pace Fortune, sends the pair, like countless other outlaw couples, on the lam, fleeing the law and Lula's overbearing mother, Marietta. "This whole world's wild at heart and weird on top," Lula declares early on, and their highly eventful odyssey, filled with abrupt twists and detours, more than bears this out. Adapting *Dune,* with its acres of plot to summarize, was misery for Lynch. But Gifford's vivid, imagistic prose and free-form narrative were far better suited to his interests and skills. Drawn to the book's mood swings and hybrid swirl of genres, Lynch heightened the contrasts: "I just made the brighter things a little brighter and the darker things a little darker," he told *Premiere* magazine.

He kept many of Gifford's quotable lines intact but concocted backstories, distorted characters (Marietta becomes a monstrous harridan), wove in a shadowy subplot involving a crime syndicate, and slapped on a happy ending (with Gifford's approval — the writer assured Lynch that Sailor and Lula would get back together in due course). The most troubling and violent scenes — the bare-handed murder that lands Sailor in jail, one character's demise in some kind of voodoo ritual, Lula's verbal rape by the villainous Bobby Peru — are either unseen in the book or entirely of Lynch's devising. Gifford likened his star-crossed lovers to Romeo and Juliet, but Lynch imposed his own mythos, borrowing from the pop-culture icons of his youth. The film's tagline summed it up: "Elvis and Marilyn on the Road to Oz."

With its good and wicked witches, and references to Toto and the yellow brick road, *Wild at Heart* is an overt, elaborate homage to Lynch's beloved *The Wizard of Oz,* a "road movie" before the term existed. The genre, American to the bone, is closely linked to the growth of the auto industry, taking shape in the noir and crime movies of the postwar years and booming after the creation of the interstate highway system and the attendant rise in car ownership in the late 1950s and early 1960s. Its defining entries — Dennis Hopper's *Easy Rider,* Monte Hellman's *Two-Lane Blacktop* — are products of the counterculture and its hangover. Even as the genre has evolved — and *Wild at Heart* was part of a moment that found American cinema seized by wanderlust, in films as diverse as *Stranger Than Paradise, Raising Arizona, My Own Private Idaho,* and *Thelma and Louise* — the romance of the road has remained ambiguous. That strip of asphalt stretching to a vanishing point in the horizon can signify any number of things: freedom, solitude, obsession, lostness, destiny.

For Lynch, whose films return often to the hypnotic image of yellow divider lines racing by, the road represents, he told Rodley, "a moving forward into the unknown." Road movies also typically pass through what he has called "the nowhere parts of America," the outposts of society and back roads of civilization. In *Wild at Heart* Lula (Laura Dern) and Sailor (Nicolas Cage) set out from Cape Fear, North Carolina, in a Ford Thunderbird, headed for the obligatory Oz of California, though they end up detained in the Texas hellhole of Big Tuna. (Their route, which begins near where *Blue Velvet* was filmed, maps Lynch's own trajectory and his eventual shift to Los Angeles–set films.) Coming or going, defined by origin or destination, the protagonists of road movies tend to find something whether or not they're looking: a sense of self or an idea of America. Lynch thought that Gifford's novel captured the mood of the country, a time when there was "craziness in the air." Lurching from one violent spectacle to the next, the film exerts a magnetic pull on all this ambient "craziness," much like the car radio that frustrates Lula as she keeps spinning the dial to find only bad news.

If *Blue Velvet* is a wholly controlled film about some very unruly impulses, *Wild at Heart* is sheer untrameled id. Perhaps not coincidentally, it dates from the brief window in Lynch's career, with *Twin Peaks* mania cresting, when he could practically do as he pleased. *Wild at Heart* seems in many ways to have been conceived in direct opposition to *Blue Velvet*. Anxious and scattered where the earlier film was contained and claustrophobic, it opens with a close-up of a lit match and is always on the verge of combustion. Where sex in *Blue Velvet* (and most of Lynch's films, for that matter) is wrapped up in guilt and terror, *Wild at Heart* is still, apart from *Mulholland Drive*, his most romantic movie, as close as he has come to a celebration of libidinal energies.

Thanks to her role in *Blue Velvet* and others like it, Dern had become typecast as the wholesome good girl, and it took a leap of faith and imagination on Lynch's part to cast her as the drawling, writhing, permanently hot and bothered Lula. "He'll refer to chewing gum or to cigarettes, and then I know what to do," Dern told a *Premiere* reporter who was on the set. (Dern and Cage became a real-life couple, as did Dern and MacLachlan after *Blue Velvet.*) Lynch also cast Dern's mother, Diane Ladd, as Marietta. Most of the other supporting parts are walk-ons: Episodic to the point of fragmentation, the film introduces Sailor and Lula to a revolving door of threatening cartoon figures, played by the likes of a blond-wigged Isabella Rossellini, Willem Dafoe, Crispin Glover, Grace Zabriskie, and Harry Dean Stanton.

Wild at Heart is Lynch's first all-out comedy, but despite the prevailing tone of aggressive absurdity, it also contains some of his most harrowing scenes. In the most notorious one, Dafoe's Bobby Peru finds Lula in her motel room with evidence of morning sickness on the carpet. Lynchian synesthesia typically combines the visual and the auditory; here he engages the olfactory. Remarking on the smell of her stale vomit, a close-up of which opens the scene, Bobby pulls Lula close and, baring his rotten teeth, tells her, "Say 'Fuck me.'" He repeats his foul mantra over and over, until finally, as her disgust apparently gives way to arousal, she does — at which point he steps back: "Someday, honey, I will!" It's a scene that leaves viewers feeling implicated, even used, much like Lula, having witnessed an assault through language, one that is no less real for being a fantasy that ends the moment it becomes a possible reality. Almost every Lynch film is a search for precisely these fault lines, which would become even more pronounced in the later films *Lost Highway* and *Mulholland Drive,* which explicitly straddle multiple worlds.

In an earlier scene, gentler in tone though no less disturbing, Sailor and Lula are driving through the desert in the dead of night when they pass the aftermath of a bad accident. Pulling

over, they find a bloodied lone survivor, played by *Twin Peaks*'s
Sherilyn Fenn, stumbling through the carnage and searching for
her purse even as her life leaks out from the hole in her head.
She's another of Lynch's uncanny beings, almost dead though
she doesn't know it. Fred Elmes, who photographed the film, recalled it was one of the most difficult scenes to shoot because of
Lynch's insistence on near-total darkness. First they had to find
a long, straight stretch of road in Southern California where no
lights would be visible (they eventually shot outside Bakersfield
and would have to wait several minutes every time headlights
appeared in the distance). The scene was also shot with a handheld camera that had to be maneuvered through almost completely unlit areas. "It made me really nervous whether anything
at all would be captured on the film," Elmes said. "But for David
there's a lot of power to not knowing what's out there."

There were mass walkouts at every test screening of *Wild at
Heart*, which persuaded Lynch to trim some of the brutality;
the scene in which Stanton's Johnnie Farragut is tortured and
killed was longer in the original cut. "There's a magic line, and
if you cross it, you're in bad trouble," he told *Variety*. "The violence was going over the line and ruining everything." The film
had its world premiere at the exact moment of Lynch's greatest fame, midway through the first season of *Twin Peaks* (the
American Pavilion at Cannes held viewing parties of the show).
The response to *Wild at Heart* was predictably divided. "As an
Eagle Scout in Missoula, Montana, did you have such graphic
visions of violence?" Lynch was asked at the press conference.
He answered with a smile: "Even worse." When a jury chaired
by Bernardo Bertolucci awarded the film the Palme d'Or, boos
all but drowned out the cheers. "It's a true dream come true,"
Lynch said, accepting the award.

A film as excessive as *Wild at Heart* is on some level ask-
ing to be punished. When it opened that summer, many critics hastened to point out that Lynch's signatures had hardened

into shtick. Some published revisionist appraisals that detected these mannerisms across his body of work; some branded him an overly self-conscious artist, symptomatic of the plague of postmodern irony. By the time Lynch landed on the cover of *Time* in September 1990, just as *Twin Peaks* was returning for its second season, he was in danger of overexposure; the story was less about the anointment of a new culture hero than the beginnings of a backlash: "The quirky outsider is close to becoming David Lynch Inc."

In the desultory meanderings of *Twin Peaks*'s second season — produced largely without Lynch's involvement but made in his likeness — the Lynchian began to seem less like an ineffable sensibility than a set of idiosyncrasies to be emulated or parodied. The common refrain was that Lynch himself, with *Wild at Heart,* was "doing Lynch." That fall *Spy* magazine included "Lynch-like" in its glossary of new Hollywood buzzwords: "Anytime something doesn't make sense or is gratuitously bizarre, studio heads now nevertheless lap it up as being *Lynch-like.*" It was perhaps a measure of how far and how quickly Lynch had fallen out of fashion that the *National Review,* the house organ of the New Right, which had likened *Blue Velvet* to pornography, published a glowing appreciation that October. Surveying Lynch's recent output, the columnist Joseph Sobran, a self-described paleoconservative, marveled that "someone has noticed" the weirdness of American life. "Someone with a camera and an imagination and the wit to spot the specifically American expressions of it, without being anti-American in his attitude toward it all," Sobran wrote. "He'll bear watching."

Lynch had yet to hit rock bottom. That would come with his next project, a *Twin Peaks* spin-off film called *Fire Walk with Me.* Sight unseen, many detractors wrote it off as an unseemly cash-in, an attempt to milk the phenomenon for one last drop of profit. Not that anything about this endeavor seemed particularly business-minded: The last episode of *Twin Peaks* drew a mere six million viewers, less than a fifth of its initial audience, and a more commercial *Twin Peaks* film would have teased out a few of its unsolved mysteries or picked up some loose ends from its cliffhanger ending. Instead *Fire Walk with Me* was a prequel, a plunge into the show's dark heart and defining trauma, chronicling the final week in the brief life of Laura Palmer — in other words, a film predestined to end with the brutal murder of its protagonist.

"I happened to be in love with the world of Twin Peaks and the characters that exist there," Lynch said at the news conference following the film's premiere at Cannes in May 1992. "I wanted to go back into the world before it started on the series and to see what was there, to actually see things that we had heard about." He later described the film as a reanimation project: "I was in love with the character of Laura Palmer and her contradictions, radiant on the surface, dying inside. I wanted to see her live, move, and talk."

This necromantic gesture is in keeping with the temporal logic behind *Twin Peaks.* Even as it obeyed the forward momentum of the serial format, the show was always drawn to the past, uncovering secret after secret — who killed Laura Palmer? Who was Laura Palmer? — or mourning the impossibility of recovering a lost innocence. Laura had already been indirectly resurrected on the show — as her doppelgänger Madeleine, also played by Sheryl Lee, and in Donna's brief stint as a bad girl after she inherits Laura's sunglasses — and directly on the page, in *The Secret Diary of Laura Palmer,* the most intriguing and harrowing by far of all the tie-ins that *Twin Peaks* spawned at its height.

Written, in an all-too-perfect Oedipal twist, by Lynch's own daughter, Jennifer, twenty-two years old at the time, *The Secret Diary* was published in September 1990, between the first and second seasons of *Twin Peaks,* and reached number four on the *New York Times* bestseller list. It covers a span of nearly six years, from the day Laura turns twelve — the journal is a birth-day gift — until a few days before her death. (Her first diary is found early on in the show; this second secret one, given to the agoraphobic shut-in Howard for safekeeping, is discovered in the second season.) Described in a *New York Times* review as "a twisted variation on *The Diary of Anne Frank*," the book is rife with the outsize hungers and confusion of adolescence. Laura's diary includes details of her first period and her first sexual stir-rings: An erotic dream, in which a boy enters her and becomes a pregnancy, could be out of *Eraserhead*. We learn about her fa-vorite foods (including creamed corn, which would take on an enigmatic significance in the show) and hear about her lost pets (she once had a pony, which may explain the apparition that ap-pears in the Palmer living room). But from very early on — as early as the addendum after the second entry: "P.S. I hope BOB doesn't come tonight" — an unease bleeds into the girlish tone.

"I've needed to forget things for a long time now," the thirteen-year-old Laura writes. Soon she's confiding about her taste for hard drugs and rough sex, recounting orgies in the woods. A tally of people she's slept with runs to more than forty by the time she's fifteen. "I'm a cocaine addict, a prostitute who fucks her father's employers, not to mention half the fucking town," she writes at age sixteen. There are references through-out to BOB, the incubus who rapes and taunts her, whose voice invades her head and the pages of her diary. That BOB is none other than her father, Leland, is a truth hidden in plain sight here. Toward the end, a few months before BOB stabs her to death in a railroad car, Laura writes, "I think of death these days as a companion I long to meet."

Jennifer Lynch told *Vice* magazine in 2012 that as a twelve-year-old she shared with her father a fantasy of discovering "an-other girl's diary" so she could compare her feelings with some-one else's, to "see if she's afraid of the same things I'm afraid of, excited by the same things I'm excited by or if I'm weird or different." David remembered this when he was working on *Twin Peaks* and asked Jennifer to create Laura's diary, based on privileged information that he and Mark Frost gave her (including the identity of the killer). In interviews at the time of its publication, Jennifer described the writing process in terms of bodily possession. "I really did enter this other person," she said. "I knew Laura so well it was like automatic writing."

Like Laura's secret diary, *Fire Walk with Me* did not need to be sanitized for TV, and it never shies from graphic content as it digs into her troubled psyche. It was made as part of a multi-picture deal with Ciby 2000, a production company founded in 1990 by the French construction magnate Francis Bouygues, which offered Lynch a relatively low budget of $10 million but total artistic freedom. The film was announced within a few weeks of the series' cancellation in the summer of 1991 and shot that fall.

For viewers expecting to sink into the pleasures of the *Twin Peaks* universe, the movie's unsubtle opening serves as a declaration of intent. A flickering field of blue turns out, as the camera pulls back, to be static on a television screen, which is promptly smashed to bits with a blunt instrument. The first person we see, in Hitchcockian profile, is Lynch himself, back as bureau chief Gordon Cole, barking orders in an FBI office. *Fire Walk with Me* begins with the investigation into the murder of Teresa Banks, killed a year earlier under similar circumstances as Laura Palmer. But where Dale Cooper's investigation led to an ever-broadening mythology and a cozy world of everyday comforts, *Fire Walk with Me* plants itself in an unwelcoming thicket of dead ends and obscure signs. Unlike Cooper, Chester Desmond (Chris Isaak), the FBI agent on the case, is a brooding, wary sort, and the town where Teresa lived, Deer Meadow, is a mirror image of Twin Peaks, a land of hostile cretins and rancid coffee. Teresa's last known residence was at the Fat Trout Trailer Park, an ends-of-the-earth dump. "I've already gone places. I just want to stay where I am," the dazed manager, Carl (Harry Dean Stanton), tells the FBI, apropos of nothing, unless he's warning the agents — and us — about the fissures that are about to form in the story.

Littered with MacGuffins and red herrings, the opening scenes seem to parody the deductive processes we have come to expect on *Twin Peaks* and from *Peaks* fans. Things that don't need to be explained are spelled out. ("M. O. — modus operandi!" Cole yells.) Basic information is conveyed in elaborate code. Cole summons Desmond to an airfield where Lil, a squinty, red-wigged woman with a blue rose pinned to her red dress, pops out in front of a yellow plane and performs a pantomime as Lynch holds four fingers to his face. Desmond interprets the dance for his baffled partner, Stanley (Kiefer Sutherland): trouble ahead (Lil's sour face) with the local authorities (her blinking eyes) who have something to hide (her hand in her pocket) and drugs may be involved (her tailored dress), though he can't explain the blue rose.

Lynch had always been obsessed with dualities, but *Fire Walk with Me* was his first bifurcated film; he would use this structure again in *Lost Highway* and *Mulholland Drive*. The first act starts to fold in on itself when Desmond, surrounded by ominously buzzing telephone poles, reaches beneath a trailer in search of Teresa's ring and, with a cut to black, disappears from the movie. Meanwhile, space-time impossibilities are wreaking havoc at the FBI's Philadelphia office. Cooper sees himself on a surveillance monitor, where he obviously is *not* at that very moment. Out of the elevator comes David Bowie, greeted by Cole as the long-lost Agent Phillip Jeffries. As he starts to ramble in a southern accent — "I'm not going to talk about Judy," he insists — the entire image dissolves into static, and we're suddenly amid a gathering of *Twin Peaks's* supernatural beings (BOB, the Man from Another Place, the One-Armed Man)

"above a convenience store." The Man from Another Place, con-
templating a bowl of creamed corn, calls it "garmonbozia," a
nonsense word that the subtitles translate as "pain and sorrow."
"We live inside a dream," someone says. Someone else utters,
"Electricity." When we return to Philadelphia, Jeffries is gone, if
he was ever there to begin with.

After this inexplicable electrical storm, more than half an
hour into the film, we finally get to the familiar environs of
Twin Peaks, but a sense of disorientation remains. The theme
music is slightly off: a softer, sadder arrangement. Laura's best
friend, Donna, looks different and is indeed played by a different actress (Moira Kelly substituted for Lara Flynn Boyle, who
declined to participate). The camera hovers along and behind
the girls as they walk along tree-lined streets, in an echo of the
stalking perspectives of John Carpenter's *Halloween* and other
slasher movies. The cinematographer Ron García, who shot the
Twin Peaks pilot, was brought back for *Fire Walk with Me.* In
an interview with *American Cinematographer* magazine, he recalled that the weather conditions made it hard to match the
color palette. It was gray and misty when the pilot was shot,
during a cold February, and García used filters to add warmth;
much of the film shoot, which began in September, took place
on bright days, which gives *Fire Walk with Me* its disconcerting
atmosphere of sunlit terror.

The movie grants Laura, the absent center of *Twin Peaks,*
the opportunity to inhabit a void, and the actress Sheryl Lee
seizes the challenge with a startling ferocity, in what cultural
critic Greil Marcus has called "as heedless a performance as
any in the history of film." Just as Lynch's films can be seen as
charged environments that allow parallel planes, multiple selves,
and wildly conflicting moods and emotions to coexist, Lee fashions a coherent person out of a fantasy figure who had been all
things to all people, vacillating between victim and heroine,
heartless vamp and little girl lost. Laura's innocence is what at-

tracts BOB, so she sullies it. She toys with boys, pleading to be saved, knowing she is beyond saving. *Fire Walk with Me* turns on Laura's discovery that BOB is none other than her father — which, the film suggests, is a cyclical, recurring trauma, something she learns and wills herself to forget again and again. The Laura of the film is consistent with the girl in the secret diary, which Lee read in preparation, though Lynch may not have. In a 2013 interview with a fan site, Jennifer Lynch said, "Truth be told, I don't think my father ever read the diary — which is both totally expected and a little sad."

Fire Walk with Me left audiences at the Cannes premiere, as one American critic put it, "drained and confused." At the press conference Lynch fielded one uncomprehending question after another. One journalist accused him of harboring a puritanical streak; others asked about the violence, the portrayal of drug use, and the sadism of the premise. Lynch was his usual tight-lipped self: "If we didn't want to upset anyone, we would make films about sewing, but even that could be dangerous." When the film opened three months later, the viciousness of the reviews surpassed those of *Dune*. "It's not the worst movie ever made; it just seems to be," Vincent Canby wrote in the *New York Times*. "Its 134 minutes induce a state of simulated brain death . . ." Quentin Tarantino, never one to keep an opinion to himself, told an interviewer: "David Lynch has disappeared so far up his own ass that I have no desire to see another David Lynch movie until I hear something different." *Fire Walk with Me* was a commercial flop, grossing less than half of its budget at the U.S. box office.

It did not help the film's commercial prospects that its version of events was considerably grimmer than the show's. The revelation that Leland killed Laura was horrifying, but it was also more or less explained as a case of demonic possession: BOB made Leland do it. When Sheriff Truman questions this supernatural account, Agent Cooper responds: "Is it easier to believe a man would rape and murder his own daughter? Any more comforting?" *Fire Walk with Me* encourages us to consider the less comforting alternative. BOB and his ghostly cohorts float through the movie, but the raw emotional realism of the domestic scenes leave wide open the possibility that BOB was a projection of Laura's, a defense against an unthinkable truth, and not an evil spirit who controlled her father. This strain of ambiguity would become central to Lynch's later puzzle films, which hinge on alter ego confusion, the question of where one character ends and another begins.

Revolving around one of the most famous dead girls in recent popular culture, *Twin Peaks* is a key exhibit in debates about Lynch's portrayal of women. After the first season, *Ms.* magazine published an essay titled "Lynching Women" by the critic Diana Hume George, who called herself a fan of the show but objected nonetheless to its "reptilian" sexual politics. Audience and creators alike, she argued, "got off on the sexually tortured, brutally murdered, mutilated body of an adolescent girl." Edgar Allan Poe believed that "the death of a beautiful woman is, unquestionably, the most poetical topic in the world." *Twin Peaks* the series might have gone along with that notion, but *Fire Walk with Me* rejects it. As Lee plays Laura, she is desperately alive. Some faulted the film as a cruel exhumation, resurrecting Laura only to kill her again, but Lynch's point is to show us how she lived and what she experienced. For David Foster Wallace, her transformation from object to subject was "the most morally ambitious thing a Lynch movie has ever tried to do."

Lynch has always maintained that the commercial and critical failure of *Fire Walk with Me* mattered little to him. Unlike *Dune,* this was exactly the film he wanted to make. Time has also been kind to its reputation — few movies have undergone so complete a rehabilitation. For Lynch the entire *Twin Peaks* project was a laboratory where he worked out some ideas that would define his late films. Not the most natural storyteller, he experimented here with narrative strictures and structures, and grappled with the needs of a continuing plot and an expanding mythology. He also moved toward more direct expressions of emotion. It's as if the time Lynch spent in the Twin Peaks cosmos allowed him to reduce this story to its essentials. What lingers is precisely what the Man from Another Place calls garmonbozia: pain and sorrow.

Bad Thoughts

THE IMPLOSION OF *Twin Peaks* and the back-to-back failures of *Wild at Heart* and *Fire Walk with Me* marked the end of Lynch's brief interlude of commercial viability. Out of industry favor, he also receded somewhat from public view. Separated from Isabella Rossellini, he was now involved with Mary Sweeney, who started working with him as an assistant editor on *Blue Velvet* and went on to produce and edit many of his features; they had a son, Riley, in 1992. Professionally, Lynch "felt this black cloud roll in," he said, after *Fire Walk with Me* and it didn't lift for a few years. It was a period of frustration, filled with abortive projects and curios that sank into obscurity, but in hindsight also one of regeneration — as if all the false starts only helped clarify his purpose and his sensibility.

On the Air, Lynch and Frost's follow-up to *Twin Peaks,* premiered on ABC in June 1992, a month after *Fire Walk with Me* was booed at Cannes. A sitcom without a laugh track (a rarity at the time), the show takes place behind the scenes of *The Lester Guy Show,* a live variety program airing on the Zoblotnick Broadcasting Corporation in 1957. ABC commissioned seven episodes of this Eisenhower-era *30 Rock,* which remains one of the few Lynch comedies to be actualized, as well as his only American-set period piece. Many gags pivot on the failure of language (the show's director speaks in an impenetrable accent that requires constant translation) or on the obtuseness of network executives (something Lynch and Frost knew well by then). The mode is lowbrow absurdist: Angelo Badalamenti's nostalgic saxophone theme is punctuated with a loud fart. ABC pulled the plug after three episodes; to this day, *On the Air* has only ever been issued on Japanese laser disc. The final, unaired episode, cowritten by Lynch and Robert Engels and directed by Jack Fisk, name-drops Man Ray and Duchamp and tips into all-out surrealism in its final sequence: A "woman with no name," clad in a black leotard and identified as a "downtown beatnik," leads the cast and crew in an exuberant dance routine, which culminates in an inexplicable shot of a bespectacled, bongo-playing dog.

Lynch made one more foray into television the following year, directing two of the three episodes in the HBO portmanteau series *Hotel Room,* both written by Barry Gifford. Set in 1969, 1992, and 1936, the self-contained segments each unfold within room 603 of New York City's Railroad Hotel. Each begins with a solemn and uncharacteristically verbose voice-over by Lynch: "For a millennium, the space for the hotel room existed, undefined. Mankind captured it, gave it shape, and passed through. And sometimes, in passing through, they found themselves brushing up against the secret names of truth." The critics savaged it; barely anyone tuned in.

He continued to write: One completed screenplay from this period, *Dream of the Bovine,* an absurdist farce about three men who used to be cows (a collaboration with Robert Engels), joined the long list of unproduced Lynch comedies. He contemplated a loose adaptation of Kafka's *The Metamorphosis,* long a touchstone, transplanted to midcentury America. When funding failed to materialize for a feature, Lynch kept busy with commercial jobs. He made a promo for Michael Jackson's album *Dangerous* and directed ads for Alka-Seltzer Plus, Karl Lagerfeld, an Armani perfume, and a Japanese coffee drink. He had been designing furniture casually since his art school days and exhibited some of his pieces, including the Espresso Table, Floating Beam Table, and Steel Block Table, made from stained pine and steel, at the Salone del Mobile, the prestigious annual design fair in Milan, in 1997; the tables were also sold through a Swiss design company for between $1,500 and $2,000.

The *New York Times* checked in on Lynch in May 1995, noting that "it has been very quiet out in David Lynch land." "I was working on a lot of different things," he explained, "looking for something to fall in love with." He also focused on his art career, presenting exhibitions in Los Angeles and in Tokyo. If Lynch's films grew more tonally complex with time, twisting established categories of sincerity and irony into new affective registers, the opposite happened with his studio art. Many of the large canvases he produced in the last two decades aspire to the willful naiveté of what the French artist Jean Dubuffet termed *art brut* ("raw art"), whose autodidact practitioners are said to have more direct access to their unconscious. Encrusted with rough, heavy impasto and sometimes painted with his bare hands, many depict a violent action, often pyromaniacal or sexual, against a field of primordial muck. Lynch has often said he would like to bite his paintings, and even his earliest canvases are textured, incorporating materials like cigarette butts and horse hair. In the early 1990s, the work becomes even more aggressively tactile, with stray objects like wire mesh and a chicken foot protruding from the canvas.

The brutality of these paintings and of *Wild at Heart* and *Fire Walk with Me* are perhaps clues to Lynch's mindset as the century entered its last decade. In a March 1992 interview with Kristine McKenna, he said: "We're in a time when you can really picture these really tall evil things running at night, just racing." A month later, the most violent riots in America since the 1960s broke out in Los Angeles in response to the acquittal of the police officers who were on trial for the beating of Rodney King, an incident that had been captured on videotape. Lynch also lost close collaborators during this time. Alan Splet succumbed to cancer in 1994. (Some of Splet's ashes are entombed under the sound console in Lynch's studio.) Jack Nance died in 1996, apparently from a head injury sustained in a scuffle outside a doughnut shop. There is a fault line somewhere in here, something that shifts the form of Lynch's films closer to the logic of the unconscious. *Blue Velvet* and *Twin Peaks* were detective stories, but from now on, the detectives would be the viewers and the mysteries on the screen would remain unsolved.

In the five-year gap between *Fire Walk with Me* in 1992 and *Lost Highway* in 1997, Lynch directed only one proper film. It lasts less than a minute and was made with a one-hundred-year-old camera. Reaching back to the earliest days of cinema, it was also a sign of things to come.

The centenary of cinema in the mid-1990s was an anxious moment for an art form and technology that many had doomed to extinction from the start. Louis Lumière, who with his brother, Auguste, patented the cinematograph and held the first ever public screening of projected motion pictures in 1895, called cinema "an invention without a future." For almost its entire life, movies have been proclaimed a dying medium, under threat from the invention of sound, then television, then home video, then digital technology. Many of its greatest innovators have rhetorically called for its demise, from the revolutionary master of Soviet montage Dziga Vertov, who proclaimed a "death sentence" in the 1920s on the cinema that came before, faulting it for mixing in "foreign matter" from literature and theater, to the young up-and-comers of the 1960s French New Wave and Japanese New Wave, whose iconoclastic provocations had a distinct patricidal edge.

But the doomsaying of the 1990s, with the centennial looming, had a particular urgency. Susan Sontag, the critic most associated with the modernist art cinema of the 1960s, published an essay lamenting the demise of cinephilia, the voracious and omnivorous love of movies that nourished the cultural seekers of her generation. The visionary French filmmaker Chris Marker, who once called cinema the art of the twenty-first century, had decided by the 1990s that "film won't have a second century." Before our eyes, cinema was turning into something else altogether. Thanks to the prevalence of computer-generated illusions and animations, the privileged relationship between film images and reality no longer held. In all aspects, from production to exhibition, digital technologies were poised to displace analog, the virtual replacing the material. The future of film likely meant a future without film.

For optimists and pessimists alike, the centenary was an opportunity to take stock. The British Film Institute commissioned a series of documentaries in which filmmakers like Martin Scorsese, Stephen Frears, and Nagisa Oshima offered a personal survey of a given national cinema's first century. A group of Danish directors, including Lars von Trier and Thomas Vinterberg, issued a back-to-basics manifesto, Dogme 95, calling upon filmmakers to take a "Vow of Chastity"—only location shooting with a handheld camera, no music or flashbacks—that would purify the form. One of the more ambitious centenary projects brought together forty renowned filmmakers under the banner Lumière and Company—including Wim Wenders, Spike Lee, Arthur Penn, John Boorman, and David Lynch—to make a fifty-two-second short film using the Lumières' restored antique cameras.

The earliest films of the Lumière brothers, termed "actualities," were documentaries of everyday occurrences—a train entering a station, workers leaving a factory—that astonished audiences who had never before encountered moving images. The filmmakers who participated in Lumière and Company were asked to work under similar technical conditions as the pioneering filmmakers, with no synchronized sound or editing equipment, and were given only a small amount of film, permitting a maximum of three takes. Whatever editing they intended to do had to take place "in camera," meaning the films had to be choreographed and shot in a precise sequence. Many responded to the restrictions by producing simple Lumière-style actualities: single-take, fixed-camera pieces in which the limited duration determines the drama. Spike Lee's entry lasts as long as it takes for an infant to speak, the Iranian director Abbas Kiarostami's for an egg to fry. Lynch delivered by far the most elaborate film, a fully imagined and wildly suggestive fever dream that conjured a world unto itself, perhaps even several worlds.

The short, titled *Premonitions Following an Evil Deed,* consists of five shots. Three policemen approach a motionless figure on the ground; the screen goes dark for several seconds. A woman in an apron on a couch looks off to the side. Another black screen gives way to a scene that could be from a silent movie: A woman in a long dress abruptly rises from a bed—there are two other women on it—but before we can quite tell what is going on, the image is blotted out in a burst of white light and smoke. The next setting is even stranger and much more ominous: Several figures with bulbous heads circle a naked woman in a water tank, banging metal objects against it. The camera pans away, again before we can register the full weirdness of the scene, and a flash of fire takes us back to the living room, where the woman in the apron, her husband now visible, rises to her feet as a policeman arrives at the door.

Other filmmakers in the Lumière omnibus made distinctive, even self-referential films—Wenders's contribution is a nod to his own *Wings of Desire*—but none asserted their signatures so completely on the exercise. *Premonitions* is a startling distillation of Lynchian moods and themes: inchoate dread, sexual menace, melodramatic panic, the home as a place where bad news arrives—all in under a minute. The abrupt dislocations are central to the film's mystery and unease. What chronology and cosmology connect the disparate scenes? Do they all exist on the same plane of reality? The film's title alone disturbs the flow of time and the logic of cause and effect. (Shouldn't a premonition precede and not follow something?) *Premonitions Following an Evil Deed* sets the stage for the second half of Lynch's career. With the exception of *The Straight Story,* all the features that followed are notable for their puzzling disruptions of time and space. *Lost Highway, Mulholland Drive,* and *Inland Empire* are sometimes known as Lynch's Los Angeles trilogy. But while they are his only films set in his adopted home, it may be more accurate to think of them as taking place in the Lynchian multiverse.

Lynch's comeback project — the one his French benefactors Ciby 2000 agreed to finance — was *Lost Highway,* cowritten with Gifford, who had become a friendly acquaintance and occasional writing partner since *Wild at Heart.* As a founding editor at Black Lizard Press, a Berkeley-based imprint active in the 1980s, Gifford had played a major part in reviving the reputations of pulp fiction writers like Jim Thompson and David Goodis; his own work heightens and estranges many of their tropes, resulting in a skewed, lyrical noir Americana. Reading Gifford, Lynch declared, is "like looking into the Garden of Eden before things went bad," which makes you wonder how much of his work Lynch had read: In Gifford land, things tend to go gruesomely wrong almost immediately. Lynch optioned Gifford's 1992 novel *Night People* with an eye on adapting it — he told Gifford his daughter, Jennifer, wanted to play one of the book's lesbian killers. But when they sat down to write, both men decided they would prefer to collaborate on an original script.

As with other Lynch projects, *Lost Highway* began with a cluster of seemingly unrelated images and words. He latched on to a sentence in *Night People:* "We're just a couple of Apaches ridin' wild on the lost highway." The phrase "lost highway" sent him into raptures (he was apparently unaware of the Hank Williams song). "It made me dream, and it suggested possibilities," he said. The *Lost Highway* script preserves a single line of dialogue from *Night People* ("You and me, mister, we can really out-ugly them sumbitches, can't we?") and the pivotal situation is a Kafkaesque metamorphosis. But the galvanizing plot point is one that Lynch said came to him on the final day of shooting *Fire Walk with Me:* someone receiving mysterious video cassettes — recordings of his own life, taped from inside his own house.

Freud characterized the uncanny as a particular commingling of the foreign and the familiar, a sense of unease that involves the oddly, or perhaps secretly, familiar, "something which should have remained hidden but has come to light." The word's German equivalent, *unheimlich,* translates as "unhomely." The architectural historian and critic Anthony Vidler identifies in the uncanny tales of Edgar Allan Poe and E. T. A. Hoffmann "the contrast between a secure and homely interior and the fearful invasion of an alien presence." It is only fitting that the film that moves the Lynchian sensibility squarely into the realm of the uncanny is premised on the latent terrors of domestic space, on a home invasion of a most eerie sort. And it is doubly fitting that the home in question belongs to Lynch.

Since 1986, the year of *Blue Velvet,* Lynch has lived in the Beverly Johnson House, a pink-hued concrete structure built by Lloyd Wright Jr., the eldest son of Frank Lloyd Wright, circa 1963. Tucked into a Hollywood Hills canyon, just off Mulholland Drive, the building is a horizontal modernist box with a hint of Mayan art deco embellishments. Its most conspicuous flourishes are the lilac stucco exterior and the rows of chevrons arranged to suggest the shape of a pine tree — an apt emblem for Lynch, the son of a woodsman. When Lynch had a pool and a pool house added, he hired as the architect Lloyd Jr.'s son, Eric, who had supervised the construction of the house for his father. In the 1990s, Lynch expanded his compound and acquired two adjacent houses. One building doubles as his production office; the other one, which he later converted into a production facility with a recording and editing studio, is the house in *Lost Highway,* which he remodeled for the film, punching vertical slot windows into its facade and lengthening an interior hallway to allow for the film's repeated tracking shots down a pitch-black tunnel-like corridor.

Lost Highway was a return to first principles. Not since *Eraserhead* had a Lynch movie so completely taken up residence in someone's head. The head in question belongs to a brooding jazz saxophonist named Fred Madison (Bill Pullman), who lives in a simmering state of paranoid jealousy with his listless, possibly unfaithful wife, Renee (Patricia Arquette). That head also happens to change owners about an hour into the film: Fred, after perhaps butchering Renee, transforms before our eyes into a younger man, Pete (Balthazar Getty), who begins an affair with the dead woman's doppelgänger (Arquette again, as a blonde).

The film's structure resembles a Möbius strip. It ends where it begins, a loop that turns itself inside out as it comes full circle. The opening line — "Dick Laurent is dead," an unknown voice declares as Fred presses the LISTEN button on his home intercom — is also the closing line, this time spoken by Fred into the intercom speaker from outside the house. In between these two mirrored statements, characters are doubled, points of view reversed. On appearances alone, the square-jawed Pullman, then known mainly for milquetoast romantic dramas (he also played the American president in the previous year's alien-invasion blockbuster *Independence Day*), matched Lynch's taste in leading men. But Fred — brooding, dead-eyed, plainly capable of rage — was a stark departure from the actor's typical nice-guy roles (and from Kyle MacLachlan's eager beavers). Arquette, then newly married to *Wild at Heart* star Nicolas Cage, plays a femme fatale, an archetype defined by dissonance, never who she appears to be. Here Arquette literally becomes a different person, and Lynch further fragments her two characters by abstracting them with close-ups of their body parts.

In his essay film *Los Angeles Plays Itself*, the historian and filmmaker Thom Andersen noted that the sleek modernist homes of Los Angeles have long been the domiciles of choice for bad guys in the movies. More than a signifier of villainy, Fred and Renee's minimalist pad is a repository of malignant, mysterious forces. The trouble begins when they find, on their doorstep, a series of videotapes of the house and its interiors. The film's first third — practically wordless, submerged in darkness, confined largely to sparsely furnished rooms and passageways that lead nowhere — is a study in inertia. Ringing phones go unanswered; the characters speak in a listless monotone; on the soundtrack, pockets of suffocating silence alternate with the familiar Lynchian thrum, room tone from hell's antechamber. The film seems about to fold in on itself from sheer malaise, from the deadweight of an exhausted marriage — or maybe it's the pressure of a world about to split wide open.

Most of Lynch's late films straddle (at least) two realities, and their most ominous moments arise from a dawning awareness — on the part of character and viewer alike — that one world is about to cede to another. In *Lost Highway* the scariest sign of slippage arrives in the shape of a so-called Mystery Man, played by Robert Blake, best known as one of the murderers in the film adaptation of *In Cold Blood* (1967) and for his role in the popular 1970s cop series *Baretta*. At a Hollywood Hills pool party, as a light-jazz version of the Classics IV hit "Spooky" plays, a diminutive ghoul in white pancake makeup and red lipstick approaches Fred. Everything he says is a challenge to Fred's grasp of time and space: "We've met before, haven't we?" "At your house, don't you remember?" "As a matter of fact, I'm there right now." Fred's bewildered response — "That's fucking crazy, man" — prompts the Mystery Man to produce a cell phone. Fred calls home, and sure enough, the Mystery Man picks up, even as he's standing before him, smiling: "I told you I was here."

Lynch's bad guys have become more spectral through the years, from the flesh-and-blood Frank in *Blue Velvet* to bogeymen like BOB and the Mystery Man. But all of them wield knowledge they shouldn't have as an instrument of fear. As Lynch said of Frank: "What's scary is when someone gets your number and they seem to know you, whether it's imagined or real." The Mystery Man is a quintessentially Lynchian figure, a man from another place, haunting the thresholds between dimensions. He is perhaps also — as he himself suggests — a projection of Fred's unconscious: "You invited me. It is not my custom to go where I'm not wanted."

After the Mystery Man encounter, Fred discovers a final video in which he sees himself next to Renee's dismembered body. Charged with her murder, he lands on death row, where he's plagued by splitting headaches that eventually cause him to turn — his face blurring and stretching like a Francis Bacon painting — into Pete Dayton, an auto mechanic who lives with his parents in the suburbs of the San Fernando Valley. The second half of *Lost Highway* suggests a half-remembered version of *Blue Velvet,* pieced together from the earlier film's phantom limbs. Just as Jeffrey pursues both Sandy and Dorothy, Pete dates a girl his own age (Natasha Gregson Wagner) and lusts after an older bombshell. Like *Blue Velvet*'s Dorothy, Arquette's mystery woman is involved with a hair-trigger ogre, in this case the gangster known as Mr. Eddy (Robert Loggia), who drags Pete along on his own threatening joyride. Like Jeffrey before him, Pete discovers a seedy underworld he barely understands, here located within the Valley's thriving porn industry (which Paul Thomas Anderson would chronicle that same year in *Boogie Nights*). And as in *Blue Velvet,* the drama is essentially Oedipal, concerning the battle for a woman between a young hero and a father figure.

Gifford knew his film noir — he published a book on the subject — and *Lost Highway,* more than any previous Lynch movie, is filled with ghosts of Hollywood past. Arquette's Alice, with her blond bangs, resembles Barbara Stanwyck in *Double Indemnity* (1944); the stilt cabin that goes up in flames recalls a critical location in *Kiss Me Deadly* (1955). Renee's description of their house as "near the observatory" brings to mind the touchstone film of 1950s youth culture *Rebel Without a Cause* (1955), which stages a climactic scene at the Griffith Observatory. (Gregson Wagner is the daughter of *Rebel* star Natalie Wood.) *Lost Highway* also has points of contact with Edgar G. Ulmer's Poverty Row classic *Detour* (1945), another film that opens on a desert highway, embroils its questionably reliable musician hero in murder, and plays from start to finish like a very bad dream.

The motif of the double, cultivated to perfection by Hitchcock in *Vertigo* and so freely used by Lynch, spins wildly out of control here. The movie's subject splits in two; the object of desire is twinned; Mr. Eddy, we find out, also goes by Dick Laurent. The setting and situation strongly evoke Maya Deren and Alexander Hammid's 14-minute short *Meshes of the Afternoon* (1943), a hugely influential work of avant-garde cinema and a miniature masterpiece of sunlit surrealism, dense with proliferating doppelgängers and dreams within dreams. Lynch claims never to have seen it, but the echoes are uncanny: even the view of the street below from Fred and Renee's living room mirrors the one from Deren and Hammid's Hollywood Hills bungalow, where they shot *Meshes.*

The critic Parker Tyler noted that many American experimental films of the mid-20th century, including *Meshes,* treated "action as a dream and the actor as a somnambulist." The historian P. Adams Sitney later classified such works, which strive to capture and sometimes induce an experience beyond conscious thought and everyday reason, as "trance films." The designation applies to many defining works of the avant-garde — by Kenneth Anger, Stan Brakhage, and others — but it is rarer to find a trance film in the form of a commercial narrative feature like *Lost Highway*. The movie's oneiric properties derive in part from its simultaneous vagueness and specificity. The repeated plunges into darkness, the drowsy trysts and aimless phone calls, all start to bleed into one another, even as characters wander into conspicuously numbered rooms and cite exact addresses (on Hollis, Garland Avenue, Deep Dell Place). Place is always precisely delineated in Lynch — announced in his titles (*Twin Peaks, Inland Empire*) and in the close-ups of street signs in *Blue Velvet* and *Mulholland Drive* — but rarely to help orient the viewer. If anything, the abundance of signposts only makes the ultimate loss of bearings all the more unnerving. (Something analogous often happens when Lynch himself speaks — he has a habit of embedding specific dates and names amid the usual nebulous stream.)

Befitting its schizoid protagonist, *Lost Highway* is a film of violent extremes. Enveloping darkness gives way to flaring, overexposed white-outs. Dead air alternates with the belligerent soundtrack assault of metal-industrial bands like Nine Inch Nails and Rammstein. (Shock-rocker Marilyn Manson, then at the height of his infamy, also makes a cameo as a porn actor.) The dreamlike sense that everything is happening at a remove dovetails with the fixation on mediation. From the opening intercom message — which Lynch says he lifted, word for word, from an actual event that he still can't explain — the film's pivotal revelations and reckonings all happen through one medium or another: over the telephone, in photographs, on videotapes and camera monitors, which may explain Fred's uneasy relationship with recording devices. Not only do cameras not lie, they have the chilling ability to register hidden urges and unspoken truths.

As in *Eraserhead,* the clammy claustrophobia of *Lost Highway* is linked to a bleak view of male sexual anxiety. Lynch later revealed that the film's basic drives — murderous jealousy and repressed guilt — emerged from a fascination with the O. J. Simpson case, the major tabloid story of the mid 1990s. In a video interview for the French DVD release, he said: "Here's a guy who — at least I believe, you know — committed two murders and yet is able to go on living and speaking and, you know, doing and golfing... How does the mind protect itself from that knowledge and go on?" The circularity of *Lost Highway* extends beyond the film: In May 2001, Robert Blake was arrested for the murder of his wife, Bonny Lee Bakley, who died of a gunshot to the head while sitting in their car. Like O. J. Simpson, he was found not guilty in a criminal trial and later found culpable for wrongful death in a civil case. (Another layer of Hollywood déjà vu: Tom Neal, the star of *Detour,* was accused of killing his wife, and convicted of manslaughter.)

The O. J. mention is an unusual instance of Lynch acknowledging a current-events connection to his work. But in both obvious and subtle ways, many of his films have their antennas up for the larger forces underlying their particular eras. *Blue Velvet* is regularly called a defining film of the 1980s, keyed in to postmodern anxiety and the brittle optimism of the Reagan years. It is no less true that *Twin Peaks* and *Lost Highway* are emblematic of the 1990s, exemplary artifacts of pre-millennial America. The period of Lynch's "black cloud" was the decade of Timothy McVeigh and the Unabomber, the Branch Davidian and Heaven's Gate cults, the televised trials of O. J. Simpson and the Menendez brothers. The culture of confession and the accelerating information age created a potent incubator for apocalyptic thoughts. With the end-of-the-century panic came a surge in new paradigms of trauma and memory, new ways of understanding our fracturing realities and divided selves. The historian Elaine Showalter coined the term "hystories" to describe the narratives that underpin the "hysterical epidemics" of the late twentieth century, which in her account range from chronic fatigue syndrome to alien abduction. New dissociative disorders made their way into the *Diagnostic and Statistical Manual of Mental Disorders* (DSM), and if these hysterical outbreaks were a contagion of sorts, the prime mediums of transmission included the daytime talk-show circuit and the pop-culture imagination.

Most of Lynch's late films can be read as post-traumatic narratives. In *Fire Walk with Me* Laura Palmer's discovery that her father is her abuser surfaces as a recovered memory, a popular diagnosis in the 1980s and early 1990s often involving childhood abuse. (It would soon become a controversial one, as counter-charges of false and implanted memories surfaced.) The press notes for *Lost Highway* suggest a possible interpretation by describing Fred's condition as a "psychogenic fugue," a condition whose main feature, according to the *DSM IV,* is "sudden, unexpected travel away from home . . . with inability to recall one's past." (Lynch and Gifford claim they had never heard of the term until a publicist brought it to their attention.) Fred's inexplicable reincarnation as Pete also implies a multiple personality disorder, which was gaining ground as a legal defense in criminal cases in the 1990s.

Lost Highway marked a return from the wilderness for Lynch but it was an anti-comeback, a film made with no concessions to popular taste or industry expectations. It premiered not in the spotlight of Cannes, but at the Sundance Film Festival, where the stakes tend to be lower, in January 1997, and was rushed into theaters the following month. The reviews were mixed at best — *Variety* dismissed it as "designer noir" and the *Los Angeles Times* bemoaned its "showy nihilism" — but there was little of the vitriol that greeted *Fire Walk with Me.* In retrospect it seems like a turning point. *Lost Highway,* to borrow Maya Deren's own description of *Meshes of the Afternoon,* "externalizes an interior state to the point where it is confounded with the external one." It is where the radical expressionism of Lynch's late period begins.

If there is a single theme that dominates the second half of his filmography, it is the power of thoughts to shape the world. In a 1909 case study, Freud described a patient he called the Rat Man who believed in the "omnipotence of thoughts," in his own capacity to alter reality through mental processes alone. This kind of magical thinking fits right into Lynch's world, where the mere fact of existence, and of consciousness, can be cause for terror. The danger of thoughts is a recurring trope in his visual art. A photograph from 1988 of a figurine with a chewed-up wad of bubble gum for a head is titled *Man Thinking.* The 2000 canvas *Mister Redman* depicts a violent encounter—between the title figure and BOB, presumably of *Twin Peaks*—that a caption attributes to "wayward activity based upon unproductive thinking." In a 2013 painting *I Am Running from Your House,* a male figure is in full panicked flight, pursued by a literal cloud of negativity, which is labeled "bad thoughts." Some of the horrors in *Eraserhead, Blue Velvet,* and *Twin Peaks* may well be emanations of their characters' troubled psyches. In *Lost Highway* and after, the bad thoughts are more omnipotent. The world itself becomes a nightmare embodiment of a consciousness out of control.

Lynch's next movie, *The Straight Story,* stands out in his filmography for several reasons. It is his only film that he did not write or cowrite, as well as the only one to have garnered a G rating, for general audiences. It also bears the mind-boggling credit "Walt Disney Pictures Presents a Film by David Lynch." Adapted from real events by Mary Sweeney and her childhood friend John Roach, the film follows the journey of seventy-three-year-old Alvin Straight from Laurens, Iowa, to Mount Zion, Wisconsin, to visit his estranged brother, who had suffered a stroke. Too visually impaired to drive and too headstrong to be driven, he made the trip astride a John Deere lawn mower, to which he hitched a trailer. The three-hundred-mile journey, with stops for repairs, took him a month and a half.

Sweeney, who grew up in Wisconsin, learned of this slow-motion road trip from a brief human-interest story that circulated as an Associated Press item in August 1994, just after Straight arrived at his destination. (It ran in the *New York Times* under the headline "Brotherly Love Powers a Lawn Mower Trek.") Lynch responded to the simplicity and immediacy of the script, which Sweeney and Roach researched by driving the route and interviewing Straight's relatives (he died in 1996). Even though he wasn't the most obvious choice for such family-friendly material, Lynch agreed to direct. As Alvin, he cast Richard Farnsworth, a seventy-eight-year-old actor who got his start doing stunt work; he drove a chariot in *The Ten Commandments* and was Kirk Douglas's double in *Spartacus*. For this homey endeavor, shot chronologically along Alvin's actual route, Lynch got some old friends involved: Jack Fisk did the production design, and Fisk's wife, Sissy Spacek, played Alvin's mildly disabled daughter, Rose. He also called up the cinematographer he thought best suited to the rhythms of the trip: his *Elephant Man* collaborator Freddie Francis, eighty-one at the time.

The double meaning of the title dominated the conversation when *The Straight Story* premiered at Cannes in May 1999: How strange, went the refrain, to encounter a Lynch film devoid of strangeness. But Lynch also has a tear-jerking, sentimental side, largely unindulged since *The Elephant Man*. It also isn't hard to see how he would relate Alvin Straight — and Richard Farnsworth, who appeared mostly in westerns — to his own

Montana roots, his rancher grandfather, and his forester father, who wore a ten-gallon hat to work every day. "I think it may be my most experimental film," Lynch told the *New York Times* in Cannes. "Tenderness can be just as abstract as insanity." The reviews were almost uniformly positive. Farnsworth, whose health was failing during the shoot, earned an Academy Award nomination for Best Actor. It would be his last film. Terminally ill with cancer, he shot himself at his ranch six months later.

Normal as it seems, *The Straight Story* is an odder road movie than *Wild at Heart,* gentle and geriatric where most of the genre's entries make a fetish of youth and velocity. The landscape looks different at five miles an hour, the top speed on Alvin's lawn mower. If most road movies are prone to spasms of violence and dystopian outlooks, *The Straight Story* sees only goodness and light. Alvin may have a dark past, but the trip offers ample opportunity for the sharing of folksy homilies and the kindness of strangers. As with the burnished opening of *Blue Velvet,* this is a utopia, a fantasy, the American heartland not necessarily as it exists but as Lynch wishes it would be. As doggedly linear as its title promises, *The Straight Story* also defines itself in opposition to *Lost Highway,* Lynch's most narratively complex movie at that point. Some thought *The Straight Story* meant that Lynch had gone soft; others applauded it as a sign of overdue maturity. Both conclusions were premature. Another U-turn was just up ahead, in the form of the circuitous *Mulholland Drive.*

11

Boulevard of Broken Dreams

THE CURVING BACKBONE of Los Angeles, Mulholland Drive stretches some fifty miles along a ridge of the Santa Monica Mountains, from the Cahuenga Pass in the east to the Pacific Ocean in the west, dividing the flatlands to the south and the San Fernando Valley to the north. Completed in 1924, it is named for the civil engineer William Mulholland, who built the waterways and orchestrated the infamous water grab that, in the founding myth of modern Los Angeles, allowed an urban mirage to emerge from what is popularly, if inaccurately, called a desert. Mulholland Drive provides an ideal vantage — some 1,400 feet above sea level — from which to appreciate the sheer expanse of the city. From one of its many overlooks, the metropolis can seem both enchanted and ominous. Especially at night, the lack of streetlamps and the glimmering blanket of faraway lights conspire to make the city below all the more mysterious and apparitional. The land of opportunity that has beckoned so many dreamers is also the "dream dump" that Nathanael West described in his 1939 novel *The Day of the Locust,* one of the first, and still among the most caustic, of Hollywood cautionary tales.

David Hockney's vast horizontal canvas *Mulholland Drive: The Road to the Studio* (1980), inspired by his daily commute, captures some of what Hockney calls its "spatial thrill," the multiperspective disorientation of moving along it. Its blind hairpin turns, which make for spectacular vistas, are also synonymous with danger: An auto graveyard full of rusting wrecks sits below a treacherous bend near Laurel Canyon, known as Dead Man's Curve. A longtime haunt for trysting lovers and drag racers, including such speed-loving luminaries as Gary Cooper, James Dean, and Steve McQueen, Mulholland Drive has been immortalized in numerous movie chases (including one in *Lost Highway*). In an essay titled "Beneath Mulholland" the writer David Thomson imagines the road as a Gulliver-size Marilyn Monroe, "with chapparal, flowers and snakes writhing over her body, and mists, smog or dreams gathering in her every curve." Lynch himself has said: "You feel the history of Hollywood in that road."

Lynch's ninth feature, widely considered the masterpiece of his late career, takes its name from this storied road and opens with a nighttime limousine ride along its winding curves — the first of many signals that this will be far from a straight story. It took until *Lost Highway,* a full quarter century after moving to Los Angeles, for Lynch to set a film in California, and it was not until *Mulholland Drive,* which began as a television series, that he made a film explicitly about this world capital of self-invention and its signature industry: motion pictures.

Mulholland Drive opens under cover of night, but when we first meet its heroine, a perky ingenue named Betty (Naomi Watts), she is making her way out of LAX, wide-eyed, into the California sunshine. Fresh off the plane from her Canadian hometown of Deep River (also the name of Dorothy's apartment building in *Blue Velvet*), Betty is a familiar figure in stories about Hollywood. Los Angeles occupies a mythic role in the American imagination as the terminal point of this promised land; as popular culture knows well, there is something poignant and often desperate about the figure of the L.A. aspirant, a seeker in the country's ultimate frontier. The two heroines of *Mulholland Drive,* it turns out, cannot remember who they are. It is only apt that the Lynch film most closely identified with Los Angeles concerns amnesia (a popular film noir trope). This is a city that is often said to lack a history, although it may be more accurate to think of it as one that encourages the conflation of history and myth.

Lynch now lives in the Hollywood Hills, in one of the canyons below Mulholland Drive, a part of Los Angeles that has retained its wildness, with its bramble bushes and stray coyotes (one of which, Lynch thinks, may be responsible for the disappearance of Pepino, the dog Isabella Rossellini gave him). He arrived in Los Angeles one August night in 1970, having driven cross-country in a U-Haul truck. "It wasn't until the next morning, when I stepped out of a small apartment on San Vicente Boulevard, that I saw this light," he wrote in *Catching the Big Fish*. "And it thrilled my soul. I feel lucky to live with that light." In many of the interviews for *Mulholland Drive,* Lynch rhapsodized about that first moment of contact with the fabled Los Angeles light. "It was the brightest thing I had ever experienced. And so it was almost an immediate full-tilt love affair from then on." "It was like happiness coming into me. It was beautiful." "I feel a kind of freedom here. I love the light and it's where there's this feeling of possibilities."

It was also around this time that Lynch set up a website to house various experiments including short films and the willfully crude (in every sense) animated series *Dumbland*. For several years, one of the most popular features on davidlynch .com was a daily weather forecast. Most mornings Lynch would post a brief video of himself, usually dressed in a white shirt and black jacket, a coffee mug before him, looking out the window of his rooftop atelier. "Good morning, it's March 12, 2009, and it's a Thursday," one typical dispatch begins. "Here in L.A., mostly blue skies, some white clouds floating by, muted golden sunshine, very still, 52 degrees Fahrenheit, 11 Celsius." Most of the reports are near-identical; taken together, they amount to a celebration of Southern California's meteorological constancy as well as a deadpan joke about it.

The quality of light in Los Angeles has inspired countless tributes. It is a strong, flat, crisp light that casts the most dramatic shadows at times and attains a shadowless clarity at others. The Light and Space art movement, whose members included Robert Irwin and James Turrell, emerged in the 1960s as a distinctly Southern Californian response to minimalism and conceptualism, with work that emphasized immersive environments, sensory perception, and transcendentalist notions. It was also the light that prompted the film industry's westward migration in the early twentieth century, allowing for year-round shooting with little or no electrical lights. (The mild climate, varied terrain, and cheap labor were additional pluses.) Hollywood turned this land of eternal sunshine into an empire of signs. The city's most recognizable icon is the most curious of landmarks: a sign on a hill that originally read HOLLYWOODLAND, an advertisement for a real estate development that no longer exists. Los Angeles, as Lynch so vividly demonstrates in *Mulholland Drive,* is a city where what counts most is often what's most visible.

Before *Mulholland Drive,* Lynch had tried a few times to make a film about Hollywood. His first writing collaboration with Mark Frost, *Goddess,* was based on a highly speculative Marilyn Monroe biography that focuses on the circumstances of her apparent suicide. While working on *Twin Peaks,* Lynch and Frost also toyed with the idea of a spin-off series for Sherilyn Fenn's character, Audrey Horne, that would transplant the backwoods femme fatale to Hollywood. They planned to call it *Mulholland Drive.* Lynch picked up the idea briefly as a feature script but dropped it to make *Lost Highway.* It was his agent Tony Krantz, who had brokered the *Twin Peaks* deal with ABC, who again broached the subject of a TV series with Lynch in the late-1990s.

When I interviewed Lynch in 2001, upon the completion of *Mulholland Drive* as a film, he explained why he had returned to television despite his emphatic disavowals of the medium after *Twin Peaks* and *On the Air.* "I'm a sucker for a continuing story, so I went there again, knowing the negative side," he said. "I just wanted to enter into a world longer." The French filmmaker Jacques Rivette once said that for all storytellers, "Scheherazade is our patron saint." When Lynch says, "Endings are terrible things," he also — perhaps unwittingly — invokes the mythic queen of *One Thousand and One Nights,* who perfected the art of the cliffhanger as a hedge against death. In its way, the circular *Lost Highway* was an attempt to make a film without a conclusion, and serial television, regardless of its risks and constraints, allowed him to defer, at least for a time, those terrible endings.

In August 1998, Lynch and Krantz met with Jamie Tarses, the youngest ever — and partly for that reason, perpetually embattled — president of ABC Entertainment, to pitch *Mulholland Drive.* Despite the network's rocky history with him, the new executives were keen to hear what Lynch had in mind. *The Straight Story,* which he was then completing, was being distributed by Touchstone, a division of Disney, ABC's parent company. There was also widespread recognition in the industry that *Twin Peaks,* despite its unhappy demise, had paved the way and whetted appetites for the 1990s cult hits *The X-Files* and *Northern Exposure.*

The two-page treatment that Lynch pitched to ABC ended up as the first few minutes of the pilot and eventually the movie. Headlights illuminate a street sign: MULHOLLAND DR. As a black limousine pulls over, the two men in front turn to face the sultry brunette in the backseat. The driver produces a gun. Hotrodding teenagers come speeding around the bend and slam into the limo. The men are killed; the woman emerges from the crash and stumbles down the hill toward the lights of Hollywood. She enters an unlocked apartment, with no memory of who she is. The next day, the apartment's new tenant, a blond aspiring actress, shows up, and — unperturbed by her discovery of a naked stranger in the shower — resolves to help her new friend solve the mystery of her identity.

The executives were hooked right away, and Lynch told them they would have to buy the pitch to find out what happens next. Most dramatic pilots are an hour long, and at the time, the most expensive ones topped out at $2 million. In a measure of its enthusiasm for the project — or its confidence in Lynch as a brand name — the network agreed to a $7 million budget for a two-hour pilot: $4.5 million from ABC and $2.5 million from Touchstone, which stipulated that Lynch shoot additional footage to fashion the pilot into a feature film that could be theatrically released abroad, as he had done with the *Twin Peaks* pilot.

In January 1999, Lynch sent ABC a ninety-two-page script, fleshing out the sketch he had sold. If *Twin Peaks* relied on a central whodunit that left a gaping hole once it was solved, he made sure this time to set enough narrative engines in motion. At the forefront is the developing relationship between Betty and the mystery amnesiac who calls herself Rita (deciding on the name when she glimpses a poster for *Gilda,* the 1946 film noir starring Rita Hayworth). A prominent subplot involves a petulant hotshot director named Adam, under pressure from sinister producers to cast an actress of their choice in his new film.

Within days of being green-lighted, *Mulholland Drive* was being hyped in the press by the chairman of ABC Entertainment as *Twin Peaks II* — he was careful to add that Lynch "has it really mapped out" this time. Shooting started in late February 1999, with Peter Deming serving as cinematographer (he also worked on *Lost Highway*) and Lynch's old friend Jack Fisk as production designer. "The fact that we were shooting for television didn't come into play," Deming told me. "As far as we were concerned we were making a David Lynch movie." Various Lynch regulars and associates had cameo-size walk-ons: Michael J. Anderson, who played the dancing dwarf in *Twin Peaks,* as a wheelchair-bound studio boss; *Wild at Heart* producer Monty Montgomery as a menacing oracular figure in a cowboy hat; Angelo Badalamenti as a mobster film financier.

For the main roles, constrained by having to cast actors who could commit for the long haul, Lynch used relative unknowns and, as always, made his selections based on headshots and informal conversations. As Betty, he cast the Australian actress Naomi Watts, who had landed only a few bit parts since moving to Los Angeles in the early 1990s. Rita was played by Laura Elena Harring, a Mexican-born former Miss U.S.A. who had mostly worked in TV. For Adam, Lynch chose Justin Theroux, then a supporting actor in indie films who had something of Kyle MacLachlan's ability to appear at once goofy and suave.

Even among his collaborators, Lynch declined to discuss plot developments, which left them wondering how the series would evolve. The pilot offered ample evidence that things were not quite as they seemed. A traumatic episode of déjà vu plays out at a Sunset Boulevard diner: One man tells another about a recurring nightmare in which he senses a malevolent force behind that very place ("He's the one who's doing it") . . . only to have that same nightmare come immediately to life. (The dirt-caked hobo who materializes from behind the Dumpster is one of Lynch's most terrifying inventions, a demonic manifestation of the urban fears that have been evident in his work since *Eraserhead.*) There are also subtler dissonances throughout. Hollywood ghosts abound — Ann Miller, the tap-dancing star of classic MGM musicals, plays Betty's landlady — as do persistent anachronisms. The film-within-the-film that Adam is directing appears to be a doo-wop musical. Betty, whose big break was winning a jitterbug contest in her hometown, projects a Doris Day naiveté, not to mention some of Lynch's gee-whiz affect.

In an interview with the *Village Voice,* Watts described her first reaction to the relentlessly upbeat Betty. "I thought, My god, this is a really one-dimensional character," she said, adding, "She doesn't belong in a story—she belongs on the side of a cereal box in 1952!" But the crew members who had worked with Lynch sensed a twist looming. Deming recalls: "We would look at David and say, 'Something bad's going to happen, isn't it?' And he would just sit there and take a puff of his cigarette and a drink of his coffee and not say a word."

Though Lynch's cast and crew were willing to trust him, the network suits were much warier. At a preliminary meeting before the shoot, the queries kept coming. How were the characters connected? Who was Rita, and how would her relationship with Betty develop? Lynch assured ABC executives that Rita's identity would be revealed in due course and that more mysteries would spring from that revelation. They questioned Lynch's casting decisions: Watts, then thirty, and Harring, thirty-four, seemed too old. When the dailies came in from the shoot, buyer's remorse started to set in. Lynch was annoyed that the executives were evaluating unscored, unedited raw footage, especially given the importance of music and sound design to his films. As he feared, what they saw only made them more nervous. The pace, slower than it had seemed on the page, was positively glacial for television. When the network's standards-and-practices department weighed in, the requests got even more inane. They asked him to cut out a close-up of dog feces and, after some back-and-forth, acquiesced as long as it didn't occupy more than one-eighth of the screen. They also stipulated that only negatively portrayed characters could be seen smoking.

Lynch turned in a first cut that was just over two hours, hoping that ABC would grant him a longer time slot. (A pilot in a two-hour slot has to be under ninety minutes to accommodate commercials.) The executives responded with a thirty-point memo of suggested cuts and tweaks. Incensed but determined to keep the project alive, Lynch and Mary Sweeney hunkered down for an all-night editing session, removing entire scenes and trimming the cut down to eighty-eight minutes: a "garbage-compactor thing," as Lynch later described it, "a butcher job." Lynch claims he never studied the ABC memo, but most of its demands were met. The spooky diner scene was gone, and the slower, more atmospheric passages had been excised.

Lynch turned his attention to the Cannes Film Festival, where *The Straight Story* would be showing in competition. Despite the difficulties with ABC, he and Krantz were still expecting *Mulholland Drive* to be picked up, if not for the fall then at least as a midseason replacement. In early May, he was quoted in a *New York Times* article about television depictions of Los Angeles, enthusing about the "different moods" he would get to explore with his new series: "The Valley is so different from Santa Monica, which is so different from Pomona or Riverside. It sort of excites me to deal with the specific moods here." ABC heads were due to unveil the network's fall lineup in late May at what the industry calls an up-front presentation, before an audience of advertisers in New York. Five days before the announcement, Krantz heard from the network's vice president of drama programming, who informed him that they were passing on *Mulholland Drive*. When Lynch got the call from Krantz, he was in the bathroom, getting ready to leave for the airport to catch a flight to France.

On the publicity rounds for *The Straight Story* that fall, Lynch faced repeated questioning about *Mulholland Drive.* He gave no indication that he was planning to salvage it. "When something is over, it's over," he told one interviewer. The *New Yorker* had assigned an article on the making of *Mulholland Drive,* which turned into an account of the clashes between ABC and Lynch. The piece, by Tad Friend, was sympathetic to Lynch, and made the point that there was no room for remotely adventur-

ous art in the craven medium of broadcast television. The last
thing ABC needed was more negative publicity. The network
was losing viewers, stuck in third place behind NBC and Fox
among the prized demographic of young adult viewers. In response to a reorganization of the network's entertainment division by Disney, Tarses resigned in August. The Thursday-night
prime-time slot that many had expected to go to *Mulholland
Drive* was filled by *Wasteland,* a twentysomething ensemble
dramedy by Kevin Williamson, the creator of *Dawson's Creek.* It
was canceled after three episodes.

For Lynch the first step was to get *Mulholland Drive* back
from ABC, which planned to air it as a TV movie in the spring
of 2000. It pained him that there were hundreds of bootleg cop-
ies of the eighty-eight-minute pilot floating around; the idea
that millions would see it was intolerable. He began proceed-
ings with the Directors Guild of America to have his name
taken off the project. A financial savior emerged in the form of
the French company StudioCanal, which had coproduced *The
Straight Story.* StudioCanal's Pierre Edelman visited Lynch in
Los Angeles in the summer of 1999 and, after seeing the pilot,
offered to buy the rights from ABC and put up another $7 mil-
lion for a follow-up shoot so he could turn it into a stand-alone
feature. Even as Lynch said yes to Edelman's offer, he was pri-
vately anxious. He had agreed to produce a feature for overseas
distribution, which would simply be a modified version of a TV
pilot, requiring at most some semblance of a poetic conclusion,
not logical closure. The whole point of a pilot was that he had
no idea how it would end.

The solution came to him while meditating, in a half-hour
session that flooded his mind with ideas that, he said, "changed
how I saw stuff that had been shot." The experience of watching
Mulholland Drive the movie involves a similarly dizzying shift
in perspective. For the first two-thirds of its 147 minutes, it unfolds more or less as the pilot would have (in Lynch's preferred

version). But the final third sabotages the primary narrative by reshuffling the deck. Watts, who up to that point has played Betty as an aw-shucks naif, is suddenly almost unrecognizable as an embittered struggling actress named Diane Selwyn. Rita is now the glamorous Camilla Rhodes, Adam's lover and muse, and Diane's ex. (Camilla Rhodes, in the first section, is the name of the blond starlet whom Adam is forced to cast by the mobsters who repeatedly and ominously tell him, "This is the girl." In the second section, it is what Diane tells a hired gun when she orders a hit on Camilla.) Most of the actors reappear, playing different characters: Ann Miller is no longer Betty's snooping landlady but Adam's catty mother; a woman we thought might have been Rita's neighbor turns out to be Diane's ex-lover; the old couple who walk a wide-eyed Betty out of LAX are shrunken taunting figures of Diane's imagination who ultimately drive her to put a gun to her head.

Lynch thinks that this is not how *Mulholland Drive* the TV series would have evolved. "The ideas that came in wouldn't have occurred if it had been done a normal way, so ABC did me a huge service by allowing it to go that way and then killing it," he told me. But the evidence suggests that Lynch was preparing to create a rupture point within the narrative, as he had done with *Lost Highway*. While he had made no mention in his story meetings with ABC of alternate worlds and doppelgänger alter egos, he had assured the network that there would be, in the parlance of Hollywood scriptwriters, "character development," and that Betty and Rita would have opposite trajectories, Betty losing her innocence and Rita finding redemption. The biggest sign that Lynch had convolutions in mind was his decision to stage a sequence in a baroque nightclub called Silencio, which is to *Mulholland Drive* what the Red Room is to *Twin Peaks,* a space of cosmic disruption and transgression where identities slip and realities multiply. Silencio doesn't appear in the pilot script, but Lynch planned to use the scenes shot here—as with the Red Room — for the ending of the feature version of the pilot, and eventually in the series proper.

The Club Silencio sequence is essentially an extended performance — a kind of metaphysical cabaret, with a magician-emcee onstage and a blue-haired lady watching in the wings — that shakes Rita and (especially) Betty to the core of their beings. The women watch as an emcee repeatedly announces, "*No hay banda* [There is no band]," . . . "And yet we hear a band." We hear music but the musicians are not performing. A singer (Rebekah Del Rio) takes to the stage and begins a wrenching a cappella performance. In a nod to the multiculturalism of Los Angeles — a defining characteristic of the city that more often than not remains offscreen — the song is "Llorando," a Spanish version of Roy Orbison's "Crying" (which Lynch was planning to use in *Blue Velvet,* though he eventually substituted another Orbison number, "In Dreams"). The song also evokes the Medea-like weeping woman of the Mexican folk tale *La Llorona,* trapped in a purgatory between life and death — a condition that will turn out to have some relevance in *Mulholland Drive.*

As she reaches the song's emotional peak, Del Rio crumples to the floor. But her voice continues. And Rita and Betty, huddled together and weeping, experience this display of falsity as a kind of visceral truth. The trick that is being undone here — synchronized sound and image — lies at the very heart of cinematic illusion, and it lends a particular piquancy to the location, the Tower Theater in downtown Los Angeles, one of the city's oldest movie houses, which hosted the L.A. premiere in 1927 of *The Jazz Singer,* the first feature to include scenes of synchronized dialogue.

Mulholland Drive becomes a film about its heroine's fragile selfhood. The first serious intimations of this crisis — of an illusion unraveling itself — arrive a few scenes before Silencio, in a less obviously Lynchian context, at an audition that Betty's aunt has secured for her. The scene is so powerfully disorienting in part because Lynch sets it up for throwaway satire. We see Betty rehearsing her lines at home with Rita, who reads woodenly from a script. Betty, on this evidence, isn't much of an actress — her idea of intensity (the scene depicts a quarrel that escalates to a murder threat) is simply to italicize her usual chipper delivery. And the scene she's reading is irredeemable: an overheated stew of soap opera hysterics that even our cornball ingenue recognizes as "lame." At the Paramount lot the next day, as Betty is ushered into a roomful of jaded industry types, failure seems inevitable — especially when she's saddled with a leathery leading man named Woody (Chad Everett) and a pompous director who gives her some tautological advice: "Don't play it for real until it gets real."

But that turns out to be the point of the scene, which "gets realer" than we could have expected. The lecherous Woody begins by leaning into Betty, turning what she had deemed a fight scene into a love scene. Betty, pushing him away, looks uncomfortable, or is perhaps acting that way. It doesn't matter — her response is in keeping with Woody's lead. "Acting is reacting," Woody tells the director just before launching into the scene. But acting is also a tricky mix of pretending, imagining, persuading, and believing — all of which Betty, who until a moment ago had seemed practically bereft of an inner life, suddenly seems to have mastered.

Grabbing Woody's hand as he goes in for a grope, Betty simultaneously takes control of the scene. She recasts herself as the sexual aggressor, whispering into Woody's ear and initiating passionate kisses. In place of simpering coyness, this Betty is all animal calculation and predatory poise. Nothing we had seen of her, as an actress or a person, has suggested she could summon such depths of feeling, let alone to such sly effect. The same could be said of Naomi Watts, who has until that point sustained a ruthlessly one-note performance. In a neat palimp-

sestic effect, Betty's unlikely transformation coincides with the
then unknown Watts's dramatic emergence as a performer to be
reckoned with. Against the odds, character and actress redeem
the "lame" melodrama of their assigned lines, infusing them
with authentic pain and even danger. By the end of the scene,
Betty has attained an utterly convincing state of hatred and
woe — to the point that Woody, locking eyes with her, recoils
as if stung. More than credible, this performance may have been
too believable.

The room reacts with stunned applause, and the film returns to the safe haven of humor: We laugh at the sheer improbability of Betty's triumph. But we also suspect that something
queasily momentous has occurred, that the film itself has been
knocked off its axis. Where did this knowing, smoldering vamp
come from? How did Betty become so self-possessed? Maybe
her self-possession is to be understood literally — as in, possessed
by a different self. This pivotal scene and the later one at Silencio suggest one possible interpretation of *Mulholland Drive* —
as a reflection on the pleasures and risks of believing in an illusion, be it movies or love. These are mysteries at the heart of so
much great art, and certainly of Lynch's cinema of emotional extremes: Through what strange alchemy does artifice beget feeling? How can something so plastic also be so profound? When
does fake become real?

Mulholland Drive had its premiere at the Cannes Film Festival in May 2001. Lynch had a generally excellent track record
at Cannes, but the last time he made a challenging film, *Lost
Highway,* the critical response had been sharply divided. *Mulholland Drive,* a nonlinear movie that requires the active participation of the viewer, was not an easy proposition in the cir-
cus-like atmosphere of Cannes, an arena of snap judgments
where movies that are not instantly digestible are often ignored
or pilloried. Most critics were admiring but also claimed to be

mystified. (*Variety* proclaimed it "compelling but intentionally inscrutable.") The jury, led by the actress and director Liv Ullmann, awarded the best director prize jointly to Lynch and Joel Coen (for *The Man Who Wasn't There*). The critical line from Cannes — that *Mulholland Drive* was beautiful but baffling — carried through to its U.S. premiere, at the New York Film Festival in October. Lynch was by then getting exasperated with questions about how the feature differed from the pilot; he didn't want people thinking of the film as a salvage job. "It's a *putrefecation* [*sic*] of the mind to talk about it," he declared at the New York press conference.

Still, the film's widely documented backstory opened Lynch up to questions about process, and he replied candidly at times. "When the new ideas came in, we went to work on it as if it were a new thing," he told *Newsweek*. "But because it started one way, it became like a tricking of the mind. Like the surrealists throwing words in the air and letting random acts dictate something." Some reviewers had trouble with the film's convolutions — Rex Reed's hysterical screed in the *New York Observer* pronounced it "a load of moronic and incoherent garbage" — but many others were happy to apply close scrutiny. Audiences who responded to *Mulholland Drive* loved it precisely for its unique architecture as a puzzle movie that required some degree of assembly in the viewer's head. The online magazine *Salon* ran a piece titled "Everything You Were Afraid to Ask about *Mulholland Drive*," untangling the film's narrative threads and mapping out its cosmology; various websites, some maintained to this day, went even deeper, parsing the significance of minor characters and the symbolism of individual objects.

The cult that emerged around *Mulholland Drive* bespoke a participatory engagement with fiction, a collective hunger — to solve, decode, demystify — that Lynch had tapped into with *Twin Peaks*. Serial narratives grew ever more popular on television after *Twin Peaks*, and viewers tended to be most fanatical when the intricate plots stemmed from larger underlying mysteries, as with the conspiratorial intrigue of *The X-Files* (1993–2002) or the shaggy-dog mythology of *Lost* (2004–2010). Fractured, elliptical stories were not new to cinema — they were in fact the stock in trade of modernist giants like Alain Resnais and Michelangelo Antonioni — but *Mulholland Drive* coincided with a mounting appetite for narrative complexity. Audiences were by then accustomed to the shifting time signatures of Quentin Tarantino's movies, or to the gentler fissures in the films of the Polish director Krzysztof Kieslowski, who explored the cosmic patterns of interlocking lives in *The Double Life of Veronique* (1991) and the *Three Colors* trilogy (1993–1994). The rug-pulling trickery of hits like *The Usual Suspects* (1995) and *The Sixth Sense* (1999) popularized the notion of narrative as a game; Christopher Nolan's reverse-chronology *Memento,* another amnesia neo-noir, was released several months before *Mulholland Drive,* and temporal loops were becoming an increasingly common device, in such films as *Donnie Darko* (2001), *Primer* (2004), and *Déjà Vu* (2006).

A movie of its moment, *Mulholland Drive* proved to be Lynch's best-reviewed film since *Blue Velvet.* Year-end critics' polls in the *Village Voice* and *Film Comment* named it the best film of 2001. Despite an underwhelming domestic gross of $7 million, it earned Lynch an Academy Award nomination for Best Director, his third; as with *Blue Velvet,* it was the film's only nomination. The acknowledgment spoke to Lynch's stature as a respected Hollywood elder, albeit one who often operates on its margins, and to the power of *Mulholland Drive* as an industry fable — the ultimate expression of Lynch's deep love-hate relationship with Hollywood.

Lynch has described Los Angeles in baldly romantic terms, as a place where "the golden age of cinema is still alive," lingering on in "the smell of jasmine at night." One of the first things he did while exploring Los Angeles was look for the driveway that William Holden's character, on the run from repossessors, swerves into in Billy Wilder's *Sunset Boulevard* (1950), setting in motion a fateful encounter with the phantoms of silent-era Hollywood. (Lynch remembers being distressed when he found out that Norma Desmond's mansion, owned by the Getty family and long since demolished, was actually on Wilshire Boulevard.)

Like Lynch's beloved *Sunset Boulevard*, *Mulholland Drive* is narrated by a protagonist who turns out to be dead. Lynch pays pointed homage with a shot of the iconic Paramount Studio gates, which were seen in *Sunset Boulevard;* parked in the lot is a 1929 Isotta Fraschini, the car Holden's character drove in the Wilder movie.

Although steeped in the romance of a bygone Hollywood, *Mulholland Drive* throws in its lot with the city's unhappy ghosts, spinning a cautionary tale around an actor's professional and romantic disillusionment. "The actor's life is one of the hardest lives," Lynch told me in 2001. "They only have themselves and they are mostly waiting and hoping, and you see how fate plays such a role in who rises and who falls." Hovering over the story of Diane/Betty are gruesome real-life antecedents like Marie Prevost, a Canadian-born silent-film actress whose body, riddled with teeth marks from her pet dachshund, was not found for several days after her death from malnutrition; Peg Entwistle, a minor stage and screen star who, legend has it, killed herself by jumping off the Hollywood sign; and even Marilyn Monroe, found dead on her bed in a fetal position, much like the body that Betty and Rita discover and that turns out to be Diane. (*Mulholland Drive,* as it happens, is dedicated to a woman who died too young: an aspiring actress named Jennifer Syme, who worked for a spell as a production assistant for Lynch, and was killed in a car crash in 2001.)

Mulholland Drive's biggest structural debt is to Hitchcock's *Vertigo,* something of a lodestar for Lynch, and the most famous twice-told tale in all of cinema. Like *Lost Highway, Mulholland*

Drive assumes the form of "a free replay," to borrow the title of an essay by Chris Marker on *Vertigo*. "You're my second chance, Judy," *Vertigo*'s hero, Scottie (James Stewart), tells the woman (Kim Novak) he has remade in the image of his lost obsession, as he drags her to the top of the tower where history will repeat itself. The notion of the second chance, the fresh start, looms large in the American imagination, as does the quest for the perfect replica, realer than the real thing, a compulsion that Umberto Eco, in his 1986 essay "Travels in Hyperreality," dubbed "reconstructive neurosis." *Mulholland Drive,* reconstituted from the ruins of an abandoned project, represents a triumphant second chance, but the story it tells is of a botched reenactment, rooted in a doomed yet irresistible urge to rewrite the past.

In the most popular interpretation of the *Mulholland Drive* puzzle, the final third redefines the rest of the film as a deathbed fantasy: eruptions from the disintegrating psyche of the heartbroken Diane, who has had her lover, Camilla (or Rita, as we know her), killed and who is herself now on the verge of death. Betty is Diane's wish-fulfilling alter ego, born of a volatile combination of guilt, grief, jealousy, and lust. Perhaps because he arrived at the finished film by working backward, or perhaps because he is naturally inclined to complicate the relationship between reality and fantasy, Lynch presents the so-called fantasy (the stuff of the pilot) as more or less realistic; the nominal reality (from the second shoot) takes the form of disjointed fragments and unfolds according to the logic of a nightmare.

If the film resonates long after these questions have been answered, it is because they are somewhat beside the point. Much more than an enigma to be cracked, *Mulholland Drive* takes as its subject the very act of solving: the pleasurable and perilous, essential and absurd process of making narrative sense, of needing and creating meaning. Whether or not they explicitly pose the question, Lynch's late films ponder the role of story at times

when reality itself can seem out of joint. Lynch's closest kindred
spirits all share this fixation, and they can be found not just in
cinema (the French New Wave veteran Jacques Rivette, the acclaimed young Thai director Apichatpong Weerasethakul), but
also literature. Like Lynch, Haruki Murakami grapples in his
books with abstract conundrums like the shape of time and the
elusiveness of the self, and understands that surrealism is at its
most effective when seamlessly embedded in the everyday. Tom
McCarthy, who blurs the lines between conceptual art and the
avant-garde novel in his work, has spoken of the "extremely literary logic" of Lynch's films, likening *Inland Empire* to *Finnegans
Wake* and the novels of Alain Robbe-Grillet. The late Roberto
Bolaño openly invites comparisons to Lynch in his final novel,
the mind-expanding magnum opus *2666,* published in 2004:
There is a cybercafe called Fire, Walk with Me and an exchange
about favorite Lynch works. *2666* is a book about literature just
as *Mulholland Drive* is a film about cinema. In both, the metaphysical terror of the void beckons just beyond the mundane
facts of the quotidian, and the relationship between dream and
reality is thoroughly rewired. By applying a fractured nightmare
logic to its nominal reality (less "realistic" than the preceding
wish-fulfilling fantasy), *Mulholland Drive* emphasizes the role
of fantasy in giving a cohesive shape to our experiences. That
this endeavor is both a refuge and a risk comes across vividly in
Bolaño's account, in *2666,* of the poet Amalfitano's wandering
mind. His "ideas or feelings or ramblings . . . turned flight into
freedom, even if freedom meant no more than the perpetuation
of flight. They turned chaos into order, even if it was at the cost
of what is commonly known as sanity." Amalfitano is reflecting
on his own mental meanderings, but he could just as well be describing the seductive purpose and the unnerving force of works
like *2666* and *Mulholland Drive.*

12

The Unified Field

A PART-TIME FILMMAKER FOR more than a decade now, Lynch has kept busy with myriad pursuits including art and music. But his most prominent role has been as a tireless advocate of the trademarked relaxation technique known as Transcendental Meditation, or TM.

The press has covered Lynch's emergence as a spiritual guru with relish — a development that, given TM's controversial history, might give new meaning to his long-held mantle of "cult filmmaker." The articles inevitably note the seeming incongruity of a creator of dark, macabre, perverse movies promoting a New Age practice that had been for decades disparagingly associated with "bliss ninnies" ("David Lynch's Shockingly Peaceful Inner Life," read one headline). But there is also an irresistible logic to the idea of Lynch the seeker of transcendence, not to mention a touch of absurdist humor in the fervor with which he has embraced his role as a spokesman for the movement, hosting fund-raisers and concerts, participating in lecture tours, and establishing the grandiosely named David Lynch Foundation for Consciousness-Based Education and World Peace. "Trying to create world peace through meditation might simply be the most Lynchian thing that Lynch has ever done," the *New York Times* concluded in 2013, in its third substantial piece about Lynch and TM since 2006.

Transcendental Meditation is not new. Among the most

popular spiritual trends of the 1960s counterculture, TM introduced meditation to the West and helped launch the hugely profitable self-help industry. The practice of mantra meditation goes back centuries to the ancient Sanskrit teachings of the Vedas. But it was the Maharishi Mahesh Yogi, an Indian holy man with an entrepreneurial streak, who simplified it for the masses — and sold it to them.

The technique, which the Maharishi developed in the mid-1950s and proceeded to promote on a global lecture tour, resonated with a quick-fix culture hungry for self-improvement: Close your eyes for twenty minutes twice a day and silently repeat a mantra to relieve stress, reduce blood pressure, improve overall physical and mental health, and even gain enlightenment. Unlike Zen or Vipassana meditation, which require mindfulness and concentration, TM is effortless. All a prospective meditator has to do is pay a fee for an initiation process, which involves the bestowal of a secret personalized mantra.

TM had its first media moment when the Beatles, well into their psychedelic phase, attended a lecture by the Maharishi in London in August 1967, at the height of the Summer of Love, and claimed they were giving up LSD in favor of "new ways of getting there." The following year, amid great fanfare, the band members and their partners — along with actress Mia Farrow, Mike Love of the Beach Boys, and folk singer Donovan — embarked on a months-long retreat with the Maharishi at his ashram in the foothills of the Himalayas. It was a short-lived infatuation, and the Beatles stormed off in a huff, reportedly over money quarrels and rumors of sexual impropriety by the Maharishi (many, including George Harrison, maintained those rumors were false). In the wake of their disillusionment John Lennon wrote an acerbic number called "Maharishi" ("What have you done? / You made a fool of everyone"), which Harrison persuaded him to retitle "Sexy Sadie."

But TM outlived the bad publicity and the counterculture,

and in the 1970s, it proved a perfect fit for the "Me" decade and its cult of self. The movement set up storefronts in many American cities, touted new medical studies that validated the benefits of meditation, and established a home for higher learning, the Maharishi International University, later renamed the Maharishi University of Management, first in Southern California and then in Fairfield, Iowa, which soon became the hub of the American TM movement. The Maharishi remained the supreme symbol of Eastern spirituality in Western pop culture, appearing on the cover of *Time* magazine and alongside meditators Clint Eastwood and Merv Griffin on Griffin's talk show.

Whether on American television or addressing followers on the Maharishi Channel, the movement's own broadcast network, the Maharishi did not exactly radiate the gravitas of a charismatic guru. A small beaming man invariably clad in white robes, a garland of flowers around his neck, he would declaim on eternal happiness and unbounded consciousness in a high-pitched singsong. The "giggling guru," as he was nicknamed, was nothing if not a Lynchian figure, a man from another place.

When Lynch talks about Transcendental Meditation, as he has done in dozens of interviews and lectures, he typically cites the exact moment of his discovery: 11 a.m. on July 1, 1973, at the TM center on Santa Monica Boulevard in Los Angeles. He had been hearing about meditation since his art school days but was always skeptical: He thought it was "mind control," "real baloney," would make him "a raisin-and-nut eater." But when his sister, Martha, a recent convert, told him about it, he detected something in her voice. Since that first vertiginous experience of "pure bliss"—like he was in an elevator and someone "cut the cable"—Lynch has not missed a session, not even during the frenzy of film shoots. He found TM at a low point—*Eraserhead* had stalled and his marriage to his first wife, Peggy, was unraveling—and he credits the practice with potentially having saved his life. "I was even thinking at the time, 'If I didn't have

this meditation, I might have seen that a way out was suicide,'"
he told the *Hollywood Reporter* in 2014. Having foresworn psychotherapy, for fear that it would restrict his creativity, Lynch
had similar reservations about meditation as a possible interfer-
ence in his "art life." Zen acceptance and enlightenment seemed
a passive thing, in conflict with the Puritan work ethic that
comes through whenever Lynch talks about his daily rituals, his
compulsion to produce. But he took so strongly to TM because,
as he would tell the journalist Claire Hoffman, "it gives you that
feeling that you could sit under a tree, but it also gives you the
feeling you could just go work." TM didn't inhibit him as an
artist; in letting him "dive deeper," it gave him more direct access to his unconscious, or, as he preferred to put it, to the ideas
swimming "out there" in the expanded field of consciousness,
where all matter is united.

Lynch was one of several million Americans who started
meditating as the TM movement crested; a Gallup poll esti-
mated that 4 percent of the population was practicing it in 1977.
(In Woody Allen's *Annie Hall,* released that same year, Jeff Gold-
blum, in a brief cameo, delivers one of the film's most memorable
one-liners: "I forgot my mantra.") Hoping to tap a Western sec-
ular demographic, the Maharishi, who had studied mathemat-
ics and physics, sought to define TM as a science not a religion,
sponsoring and publicizing numerous scientific studies on meditation. At the same time, TM initiatives became ever more gran-
diose, expanding beyond meditation instruction to a so-called
Sidhi program, an advanced technique that involved levitation,
or "yogic flying" — in effect, bouncing up and down on a mat-
tress while in the lotus position. If practiced communally and in
sufficiently large groups, the Maharishi maintained, this would
produce a surplus of positivity that would lead to a decrease in
crime, violence, accidents, even unemployment. Missionary plan
packaged as mathematical equation, the Maharishi Effect held
that if 1 percent of the square root of the planet's population

meditated, it would bring about world peace. TM continued to keep up with the times. In the rapacious free market 1980s, it was, more than ever, big business. Even as the Maharishi withdrew from public view, eventually retreating to his compound in the Dutch town of Vlodrop, his empire expanded to encompass ayurvedic health care products, a construction company specializing in Vedic architecture, multiple colleges and universities, and a political movement, the Natural Law Party, which at its peak was active in more than seventy countries.

Some disciples abandoned the organization, even while continuing to meditate in private; it was one thing to help lower blood pressure, another to pursue the goal of "world government." (The self-improvement guru Deepak Chopra left the TM movement in the 1990s, in part because of what he called its "cultish atmosphere.") Lynch remained tight-lipped about TM for many years, apparently wary of the stigma, even in fad-prone, spiritually tolerant Hollywood. "I don't really talk about meditation," he said in a 1990 interview. "A lot of people are against it. It's just something I like . . ." But over the years, as meditation moved into the mainstream, Lynch grew more open in his embrace. When the quantum physicist and TM leader John Hagelin ran for president as the Natural Law Party candidate in 2000, Lynch directed his campaign video — a strange and stilted infomercial in which Hagelin recites his positions (mostly liberal and libertarian) while posed in front of a gold curtain.

In 2001, Lynch signed up for the TM Enlightenment Course, reserved for meditators willing to pay a million dollars for the privilege of spending a month with the Maharishi. Lynch arrived in Vlodrop in June 2002 to discover that he would not be seeing his spiritual mentor in the flesh. The handful of select visitors who were admitted into his log house in the final years of his life found themselves confronting an empty red velvet throne while the Maharishi appeared on a monitor, beamed in via teleconference from his room upstairs. "When I play it back in my mind, he was right there," Lynch told Hoffman. "It's a strange thing. He was right above us but came through the television. But it was as if there was no television. And that's the way it was." The incorporeal guru calling the shots from another room: It could be an image from David Cronenberg's *Videodrome*, with its disembodied talking head, Brian O'Blivion, who exists only as a library of videotapes, or from one of Lynch's own films, the man in the control room in *Mulholland Drive*, issuing cryptic orders via intercom.

Lynch emerged from the Enlightenment Course on a high — "Everyone I saw was like a hero to me," he told Hoffman — and all the more committed to the cause. In June 2003, he participated in a press conference at the Four Seasons Hotel in Beverly Hills, where John Hagelin announced plans to build a twenty-thousand-square-foot "peace palace" in Los Angeles for communal meditation, which would face east in accordance with the laws of Vedic architecture. Lynch and several Hollywood stars, including actors who had worked with him, like Laura Dern, Heather Graham, and Laura Elena Harring, sat in silence for a few minutes to demonstrate the practice of TM.

In October 2003, Lynch called another press conference, this time at the Plaza Hotel in Manhattan, to announce his goal of raising $1 billion to build a global network of peace palaces; the Maharishi participated via satellite from Holland. "Right now, we gotta get peace back in the world," Lynch told the *New York Post*. (This was six months after the American invasion of Iraq.) A *Vogue* article described the daily ritual at Lynch's Hollywood Hills office: Every day at 5:30 p.m., computers and phones are turned off and the entire staff retreats to his soundproofed recording studio to meditate together.

Lynch established his foundation in July 2005 and went on a nationwide college tour called "Consciousness, Creativity, and the Brain" with Hagelin and the neuroscientist Fred Travis. Students at Yale, Brown, UC Berkeley, and elsewhere showed up curious for a glimpse into Lynch's creative process. What they got was Lynch talking about how meditating is "money in the bank" for an artist, a lecture from Hagelin on the relationship between string theory and consciousness, and a demonstration in which a meditator was hooked up to an EEG to show the shift in brain activity while transcending. When the Maharishi died in February 2008, Lynch joined thousands of mourners for his funeral in the Indian town of Allahabad, where he was cremated on a large sandalwood pyre overlooking the sacred spot where the Ganges and Yamuna rivers converge.

Lynch's association with the movement has not been without controversy. He visited Germany in 2007 hoping to buy Teufelsberg, or Devil's Mountain, a hill in the outskirts of west Berlin consisting of some twelve million cubic meters of World War II rubble. Under it lies a never-completed Nazi military school designed by Albert Speer; on top of it is the white-domed remnant of a Cold War–era U.S. "listening station." The plan to transform this curious site into a transcendental university ran into negative publicity when Emanuel Schiffgens, a German TM "raja," wearing a white robe and a shiny gold crown, stood before a Berlin audience next to Lynch and proclaimed, in German: "We want an invincible Germany!" He later clarified that he meant "invincible" in the sense of "free from negativity," but the damage had been done.

By and large, though, Lynch's foundation has emerged as the benign face of TM, moving back to basics and focusing on good deeds. Over the years talk of levitation and peace palaces has given way to an emphasis on the more tangible, down-to-earth benefits of the practice. While attempts to get TM taught in public schools have faced occasional resistance since the 1970s on First Amendment grounds, the Lynch foundation has had success in introducing classroom "quiet time" for students at underperforming schools. Most of its efforts are geared toward providing TM at no cost to "at-risk groups," including the homeless, Native Americans with diabetes, prison inmates, and veterans with post-traumatic stress disorder. Some credit Lynch with convincing the movement to reduce its initiation fee, which had rocketed from $75 in 1973, when he signed up, to $2,500 in 2007. It was slashed to $1,500 the following year (the recessionary economy might also have been a factor). Whether from lower cost or higher profile, annual TM enrollment has soared since Lynch launched his foundation.

Lynch's personal life entered a period of upheaval around the time he became the face of the TM movement. In May 2006, he married Mary Sweeney, his romantic partner and a close collaborator for some fifteen years, but filed for divorce a month later. He soon became involved with Emily Stofle, an actress who appeared in *Inland Empire* and who is thirty-three years his junior; they married in February 2009, and in 2011, Lynch's fourth child was born, Lula, who shares the name of Laura Dern's character in *Wild at Heart*. The *New York Times Magazine* asked Lynch about his multiple marriages in 2008: "You've been married three times before?" "Yeah, it's real great." "Why would someone who feels so blissed out marry so many times?" "Well, we live in the field of relativity. Things change."

Many of the old friends who discovered TM with Lynch in the 1970s — including Catherine Coulson, Frederick Elmes, and Jack Fisk — have continued the practice. He has introduced it to many actors on movie sets, as well as to singer Julee Cruise and cinematographer Peter Deming. (When *Twin Peaks* star Sherilyn Fenn finally tried it in 2013, she wrote on her blog: "March 24 is the first day of the rest of my life. It is changing my life in every way. DKL gifted it to me as I could not afford the amount one must pay to learn these sacred teachings.") Not everyone close to Lynch has been so receptive. Isabella Rossellini told author Greg Olson: "Transcendental Meditation gave me a headache when I tried to do it. I was raised a Catholic, and my head was already too full of rules and regulations."

Many have wondered out loud if meditation has dulled Lynch's edge or driven him to distraction. "If you're a meditator it doesn't mean that you're going to do movies about knitting," he told the *New York Times* in 2003. But in the decade since his emergence as a TM advocate, Lynch has made only one film, *Inland Empire,* his most experimental work as well as the one in which his spiritual cosmology is most apparent. He maintains he is just waiting for the right idea to come up, the right big fish. But some think he has found a higher calling. The filmmaker Abel Ferrara, in an interview with the *Indiewire* website in 2011, put it most bluntly: "Lynch doesn't even want to make films anymore. I've talked to him about it, OK? I can tell when he talks about it." He added, mockingly: "I'm a lunatic, and he's pushing Transcendental Meditation."

When I interviewed Lynch in the fall of 2006, the one subject that elicited more enthusiasm than Transcendental Meditation was digital video, the format on which he had shot his latest film, *Inland Empire.* "The sky's the limit with digital," he said, sounding at once excited and agitated. "Film is like a dinosaur in a tar pit. People might be sick to hear that because they love film, just like they loved magnetic tape. And I love film. I love it!" He contorted his face into an expression that suggested pain more than love: "It's so beautiful. [But] I would die if I had to work like that again."

Invented in the 1950s, video is an audiovisual medium based on an electronic signal, as distinct from the projected celluloid images of film. In its early years, video was most commonly used for television broadcasts and in galleries by an emerging coterie of video artists. Lynch first experimented with the format in 1974 when Fred Elmes, with whom he was making *Eraserhead,* was asked by the American Film Institute to test two types of videotape. Lynch asked if he could shoot a short film twice. The result, made in an afternoon, was *The Amputee,* a single shot of a legless woman (played by Catherine Coulson) writing a letter, which we hear in voice-over, while a nurse tends to her bandaged stumps, a process depicted in ghoulish detail. (Coulson told author Greg Olson that the AFI administrators, expecting to see a simple camera test, were appalled at the result and asked Elmes: "Did Lynch have something to do with this?")

The practice of shooting feature films on video became widespread only in the mid-1990s, with the switch from analog to digital video and with the introduction of the cheap, compact MiniDV format. The Dogme 95 movement, led by Danish troublemaker Lars von Trier, kicked off the digital revolution, and before long, DV was the default mode for indie filmmaking the world over. High-definition video, which often closely approximates film, soon became the most common format for studio productions as well. But the first wave of MiniDV films fall into two broad categories: those that treat video as a language in itself, with its own expressive potential (the first Dogme film, *The Celebration,* for instance, or *The Blair Witch Project*), and those that attempt to disguise, or neglect to consider, the video-ness of video and use it simply as an affordable substitute for film.

Lynch was not interested in simulating celluloid with a state-of-the-art video camera. He shot *Inland Empire* with the relatively primitive Sony DSR-PD150, a consumer-grade model that was introduced in 2001 at a retail price of less than $4,000. He had used the same camera to shoot experimental vignettes like *Rabbits,* an episodic series in which a rabbit-headed family recites Beckettian non sequiturs to the sound of canned sitcom laughter, some of which he posted on his website. Lynch grasped the potential of digital technology earlier and took to it with greater fervor than filmmakers half his age. He launched the labyrinthine davidlynch.com in 2001, carrying merchandise (mugs, photos, alarming ring tones) and subscriber-only content (live-action and animated shorts, original music).

Lynch's love of video has much to do with the freedom it

grants — just as painting requires little equipment beyond a can-vas and paint, shooting with a camcorder removes the strictures of a traditional production, allowing for a smaller crew, less setup time, and no accountability to moneymen. *Inland Empire* was written a scene at a time and shot fitfully over a period of three years, without an ending in mind or (to begin with) a unifying vision. The genesis was a fourteen-page monologue he wrote for his old friend and collaborator Laura Dern, in which she plays the part of a tough-talking southern dame, spilling her guts out in a dank room to an unidentified interrogator, telling floridly vulgar tales of sexual violence and terrible revenge. They shot it once, in a seventy-minute take, on a set built in Lynch's paint-ing studio. He continued through a process of free association: "I would get an idea for a scene and shoot it, get another idea and shoot that. I didn't know how they would relate." Only after the project was well under way did he contact StudioCanal, his benefactor on *Mulholland Drive*. The executives signed on even though Lynch, as he puts it, "told them two things: 'I don't know what I'm doing, and I'm shooting on D. V.'"

The title came from Dern, who had just moved down the street from Lynch. She mentioned to him one day that her then-husband, the musician Ben Harper, was from the Inland Em-pire area to the east of Los Angeles. Another piece fell into place when Lynch decided to shoot in the Polish city of Lódz, which hosted a cinematography festival that he first visited in 2000. (The festival has since moved to Bydgoszcz.) Once a world cap-ital of textile production and the location of one of the larg-est Jewish ghettos during World War II, Lódz became a hub of the film industry after the war and is home to a prestigious film school, where directors like Andrzej Wajda and Roman Polan-ski studied. Lynch loved the post-industrial city's abandoned factories — they inspired a series of photographs, which he ex-hibited in 2013 — and even announced plans (since abandoned) to build a film studio in Lódz.

Just as the structure of *Mulholland Drive*—with its decisive fault line and eureka epiphanies—reflects its evolution from open-ended TV pilot to stand-alone feature, *Inland Empire* is also shaped by the conditions of its creation. Clearly the film, which is as close as Lynch has come to the surrealist practice of automatic writing, could not have been made any other way. An experience of total immersion and continual slippage, it feels like the product of a sustained, unedited brainstorm. No waiting around for money or even for the big picture to emerge. What Lynch finds "beautiful" here is the sheer liberation of being able to work flexibly and spontaneously. The film is astonishing not least for how far "inland" it goes, for the relative absence of barriers between the director's unconscious and what he puts on-screen.

The disparate segments and parallel worlds of *Inland Empire* come together as a story of a grave identity crisis. The trouble begins when actress Nikki Grace (Dern), who lives in a cavernous Hollywood mansion, receives a visit from a new neighbor (Grace Zabriskie). With the camera pressed up against her face, she recounts, in a heavy Eastern European accent, "an old tale," a Lynchian take on the Christian fall of man: "A little boy went out to play. When he opened his door he saw the world. As he passed through the doorway he caused a reflection. Evil was born." She also offers "a variation" of the story, involving "a little girl," "lost in the marketplace, as if half-born" and a clue that "through the alley behind the marketplace" lies "the way to the palace." (In a 2008 interview with Richard A. Barney, Lynch explained that "the marketplace" and "the palace" are terms he picked up from the Maharishi: "You go through the marketplace, and it's real interesting, but there are lots and lots of chances to get waylaid and even go backwards and get lost, get in trouble." The palace, on the other hand, represents transcendence.)

As the neighbor predicts, Nikki lands a coveted role in a hokey southern melodrama called *On High in Blue Tomorrows* opposite womanizing leading man Devon (Justin Theroux). She soon learns that the movie is a remake and that the original Polish production was aborted when both stars were murdered. As film and reality violently intersect, space and time also begin to fissure. One minute we're in sunny Southern California, the next in snowy Old World Poland. (The inland empire refers as well to Mitteleuropa.) Nikki begins to merge with her character, Sue, and the script's adulterous affair spills over into real life. But what's real, and who's dreaming whom? Besides Nikki and Sue, Dern plays at least two other overlapping variations on the character: One is the vengeful woman from the initial monologue, which is carved up and strewn throughout the film. The other lives in a shabby suburban house, sometimes with a harem of gum-chewing, finger-snapping young women. The shadowy Lynchian network of behind-the-curtain dealings comes to suggestively entangle the movie industry and a prostitution ring. Periodically interspersed are non sequitur scenes from *Rabbits.* Certain phrases, often pertaining to identity confusion ("I'm not who you think I am," "Look at me and tell me if you've known me before"), repeat in varying contexts and start to acquire talismanic power. Meanwhile, the film we are watching is beamed to a TV in a hotel room, and a mystery brunette watches along with us, silently weeping.

There is no decisive rupture in *Inland Empire,* as there was in *Lost Highway* and *Mulholland Drive.* The experience is instead one of permanent free fall. If Lynch's other films have favored self-contained locales — neighborhood stories — *Inland Empire* oozes, miasma-like, across continents and even dimensions. This warren of wormholes is highly susceptible to cosmic disruption, and it takes no more than a few witchy intonations from Zabriskie, coupled with a low bass rumble, to cause the space-time fabric to fold. As with Naomi Watts's jaw-dropping audition in *Mulholland Drive,* the real catalyzing event is the first time we see Nikki act, at a rehearsal with her costar Devon and her director (Jeremy Irons). The scene is nonsense, and she's sensational. Nikki's performance is so good — so real? — that it sets off a mysterious noise in the bowels of the soundstage, the unlit corners that here seem analogous to the deepest recesses of the unconscious.

Inland Empire belongs to the lineage of Hollywood bloody valentines that runs from *Sunset Boulevard* to *Mulholland Drive*. In one scene a character, stabbed in the gut with a screwdriver, runs down Hollywood Boulevard, leaving a gory trail on the Walk of Fame. The film is at once a tribute to actors, especially those chewed up and spit out by the industry — "lost in the marketplace" — and a study of the metaphysics of their craft. It elaborates on the Lynchian notion, glimpsed in *Mulholland Drive*'s audition scene, of acting as an out-of-body experience. Dern summons an almost frightening intensity in a performance that requires her to inhabit three (if not more) overlapping parts, lapsing in and out of a southern drawl. "I thought of it as playing a broken or dismantled person, with these other people leaking out of her brain," Dern told me in a 2006 interview, adding that she thought of Catherine Deneuve's portrait of psychosis in Roman Polanski's *Repulsion*. She also said the stop-start shoot had advantages for a role like this: "It's unbelievably freeing. You're not sure where you're going or even where you've come from. You can only be in the moment."

Lynch's lurid scenarios have generally been tempered by the seductive richness of his visuals. The video murk of *Inland Empire* takes some getting used to, not least because form fits content all too well: The bleeding, sludgy palette is entirely suited to the sickened, splintering headspace that the film inhabits. Lynch makes little attempt to disguise the pixels, flickers, and shadows of the medium, and the unconditional embrace means his DV images are about as tactile as his celluloid ones. There are even several moments (on a snowy Polish street) that approach conventional beauty, and a few more — studies in extreme darkness and extreme light — that are reminders of Lynch's parallel painting career. As the film abandons narrative logic, the decision makes more and more sense. DV seems simultaneously less and more "real" than what our celluloid-conditioned eyes are used to: Video is to film as dreams, or nightmares, are to reality.

Compared with film, video typically looks harsh and almost hyperreal, with a narrower range of colors and weaker contrast, but it's precisely those qualities that Lynch revels in. While a lower-resolution film stock, like Super 8, has a grainy, romantic allure, lower-resolution video, characterized by fewer pixels per inch, usually just looks fuzzy. "Everybody says, 'But the quality, David, it's not so good,' and that's true," Lynch told me. "But it's a different quality. It reminds me of early 35-millimeter film. You see different things. It talks to you differently." Lynch's comparison of low-res video to early film stock, before the emulsion process was perfected, is instructive: The murkier the image, the more room to dream. It's no wonder this master of the enigmatic would prize video for its literal lack of information.

The DV of *Inland Empire* is the medium of home movies, viral videos, and pornography — the everyday media detritus we associate more with television and computer monitors than movie theaters, more with intimate or private viewing experiences than communal ones, which may be why the film works even better on a small screen than a big one. This lurid, grubby fantasy seems to spring from deep within the bowels of YouTube as much as from inside its heroine's muddy unconscious. Not only does *Inland Empire* often look like it belongs on the Internet, but it also progresses with the darting, associative logic of hyperlinks. It was not just digital video but digital editing that lent itself to the discontinuous worlds and fragmented psyches of *Inland Empire:* This was the first feature that Lynch cut on a computer — with editing software, in a process known as non-linear editing — instead of manually on a flatbed.

Video, as Lynch uses it here, is the language of the unconscious. Even in *Lost Highway* it was clear that, to Lynch, video communicates a different kind of truth: The tapes that show up on Fred and Renee's doorstep are not mere stalker artifacts; they signal the return of the repressed. When a detective asks whether the couple owns a camcorder, Fred says he prefers "to remember things my own way... Not necessarily how they happened." The discovery of Renee's mutilated body, not incidentally, happens on video. DV looks more lifelike than film: Its frame rate, the frequency at which successive images are captured, is higher than film's and closer to how the human eye operates. The artist Robin Deacon has said that video affords "a truer sense of what is being seen." But it also can seem unnaturally heightened to celluloid-trained eyes. Lynch uses video with the curiosity and resourcefulness of an innate visual artist. He pays attention to its flickers, its shadows, its susceptibility to distortion from under- or overexposure. Bodies and faces are repeatedly abstracted with an unforgiving lens or light source, and Dern fearlessly offers herself up to one disfiguring wide-angle shot after another. The extreme close-up is a Lynch trademark, and here, using his DV camera like a new toy, he peers at his subjects even more intently than usual, as if he's stumbled on an entirely different way of looking.

Film is a physical process, dependent on the interaction of light and chemistry. Video is by definition more remote, more spectral, a cluster of data in the electronic ether. And while mortality is a defining trait of film, a medium that degrades and disintegrates over time, video — quickly and endlessly reproducible — conjures a spooky sense of the infinite. In *Inland Empire,* truly a horror movie for the digital age, it's not that the ghost is in the machine. The ghost *is* the machine.

Inland Empire premiered in September 2006 at the Venice Film Festival, where Lynch also received a lifetime achievement award. As usual the first round of reviewers were mostly flummoxed. The *Guardian* deemed the film "inspired and incomprehensible by turns," while *Variety* called it "dull as dishwater and equally murky." A few weeks later, though, *Inland Empire* was the hottest ticket at that year's New York Film Festival: a mobbed press preview, scalpers at the public screening. Determined to maintain total control from production through to exhibition, Lynch acquired U.S. rights for *Inland Empire* from the French producers and released it that December through his own distribution company, Absurda. In New York at least, it was a hit, with hundreds turned away during its opening weekend at the IFC Center, the former home of the Waverly where *Eraserhead* once ran for months. Lynch also mounted an Oscar campaign for Dern's widely praised performance — or perhaps it was a statement on the absurdity of Oscar campaigns — by camping out on a Hollywood intersection, not far from the Walk of Fame, with a live cow and a sign that read WITHOUT CHEESE THERE WOULDN'T BE AN INLAND EMPIRE. "The Academy members love show business," he told *Time* magazine by way of explanation. "And this is show business, being out with the cow."

While *Inland Empire* was seen as a companion piece to *Mulholland Drive* — in the *New York Times* Manohla Dargis described it as an "evil twin" — it pointedly lacks the earlier film's Old Hollywood patina and puzzle-solving satisfactions. What it does is sustain and amplify the Lynchian sensation of dread to proportions never before felt. In preparation for an interview with Lynch for a *New York Times* article, I watched the film alone in his screening room in the Hollywood Hills one afternoon in September 2006, in what was once the *Lost Highway* house, and it remains perhaps the most indelible viewing experience of my life. Sitting a few seats over from Lynch's (off limits to anyone else and demarcated by a large ashtray on its armrest), reeling from the film's violent disjunctions, I found eerily plausible its contention that there could be "something inside the story," as one character puts it, something malignant and possibly contagious. *Inland Empire* is, among other things, Lynch's most effective horror movie. Cinematic scare tactics abound, in the form of portentous tracking shots, shock cuts, and loud noises. But the film's queasiest special effect is in persuading the viewer that its stories — all stories — have a life of their own, that they are spaces to inhabit, forces that haunt. *Inland Empire* opens with the light of a projector beam and a phonograph needle tracing the grooves of a record, and it constantly calls attention to its own means of production. Mediums of transmission come to seem like vessels of evil, to the point that I kept glancing over uneasily at the computer that was playing the movie off a QuickTime file.

For all the abject terror that it summons, *Inland Empire* may contain the truest happy ending in the Lynch oeuvre. *Mulholland Drive* is a more palatable film, but its reality is crueler: a dream overlaid on a nightmare. *Inland Empire* is almost all nightmare, and yet, through considerable exertions, it blinks itself awake, and into a state of grace. As the film ends, Nikki finds herself in a roomful of women (including Nastassja Kinski and Laura Elena Harring from *Mulholland Drive*) and Lynchian figures (a lumberjack sawing into a log, a monkey that might have strayed in from the last scene of *Fire Walk with Me*). The last word — "Sweet," uttered by a woman with a prosthetic leg — gives way to the rousing strains of Nina Simone's "Sinnerman." Kisses are blown; a dance breaks out. Some have read *Inland Empire* as a culminating work, and the end credits as a final bow, but it could just as well be a show of defiant jubilation from an artist who, in his seventh decade, has found new ways to be freer.

Busier than ever as he approaches seventy, Lynch remains very much a moving target, though not necessarily as a filmmaker. The longer he has gone without making a movie, the greater and more widespread the interest in him. Every glancing comment by a onetime collaborator about a potential project prompts a firestorm of online speculation. Every new endeavor is scrutinized, its meaning dissected, its place in the ever more eccentric Lynchian corpus debated.

Here are just some of the things Lynch did and said that made news in 2014: He took part in an onstage conversation at the Brooklyn Academy of Music in April. The enthusiastic sold-out crowd hung on his every word, even as audience members learned almost nothing new about him, save for his admiration of Kanye West. (The host played a snatch of "Blood on the Leaves." "So beautiful," Lynch said.) When Laura Dern, promoting a film in June, said Lynch was "cooking up" a new movie, film blogs pounced on the vague remark and treated it as breaking news. But Lynch, speaking to the *Guardian* a few weeks later, said he had "no new plans yet for a new movie" and was focusing on "a new painting."

In July, he unveiled a line of fitness wear for women: floral-print yoga leggings and tank tops. That same month, ninety minutes of previously unseen footage from *Fire Walk with Me* surfaced in a Blu-ray box set, *The Missing Pieces,* a rare DVD release that warranted a Hollywood premiere, complete with cast reunion. In August, Lynch posted his contribution to the viral social media stunt of the moment, the Ice Bucket Challenge, which required people to make videos of themselves upending a bucket of ice water on their heads and nominating others to do so, all while supposedly raising money and awareness for amyotrophic lateral sclerosis. Lynch's minute-long ALS video is an instant classic: He spikes his ice water with a double espresso, plays a few bars of "Over the Rainbow" on the trumpet, and, in a rare political gesture, nominates Vladimir Putin (who did not take him up). Commenters deemed it "very Lynchian"; someone posted a version of it unspooling backward.

On a Monday morning in October 2014 came the biggest

Lynch news in a decade: *Twin Peaks* would return for a third season in 2016, a quarter century after it revolutionized television, thus fulfilling Laura Palmer's enigmatic promise in the show's final episode: "I'll see you again in twenty-five years," she tells Agent Cooper. As Lynch hasn't directed a film since *Inland Empire,* the prospect of nine new *Peaks* episodes, all cowritten by Lynch and Mark Frost and directed by Lynch, sent the Internet into a frenzy, whipping up speculation about which actors would be brought back, how the show might account for the twenty-five-year gap, whether it would return to any of the original unsolved mysteries, and so on. Lynch and Frost declined interviews but more details soon emerged: Kyle MacLachlan was confirmed to return as Agent Cooper, and as with Laura's diary, a new novel by Frost, *The Secret Life of Twin Peaks,* would fill in developments from the intervening twenty-five years.

Events took another twist in April 2015 when Lynch announced on social media that he would not be involved in the revived *Twin Peaks.* "I left because not enough money was offered to do the script the way I felt it needed to be done," he wrote. Amid a storm of conjecture over whether this was a bargaining ploy or cold feet or yet another example of Lynch's allergy to even the slightest hint of compromise, multiple "Save *Twin Peaks*" petitions were launched, reminiscent of the letter-writing campaign to rescue the original show. Several *Peaks* actors banded together for a protest video. ("*Twin Peaks* without David Lynch is like a girl without a secret," Sheryl Lee cooed into the camera.)

The standoff was resolved a month later. "The rumors are not what they seem," Lynch wrote on Twitter. "It is !!! Happening again." Showtime confirmed that Lynch would direct the entire new season, which would now total more than the originally planned nine hours. The avid scrutiny that has accompanied every stage of the behind-the-scenes drama speaks to the void left by Lynch's retreat from filmmaking and the potency of the spell he has cast on generations of moviegoers. So many of us have had formative encounters with the Lynchian, whether we drifted unawares into a midnight showing of *Eraserhead* or watched slack-jawed as *Blue Velvet* put on-screen perversions we didn't know existed, whether we were hooked on *Twin Peaks* or stumped by *Inland Empire*.

His movies are the weird tales that give form to the submerged traumas and desires of our age, perhaps even to questions that have haunted artists and thinkers for centuries: how to explain evil, how to live with fear, how to hold the self together, how to keep reality as we know it from falling apart. These may sound like great claims to make for a movie director, but compared with almost any popular artist of our time — to put it in Lynchian terms — he dives deeper and catches bigger fish.

Acknowledgments

THERE ARE FOUR people without whom this book would not exist: James Atlas, Ed Park, James Fitzgerald, and of course David Lynch. My gratitude also goes to those who spoke to me either for the book or for earlier articles on Lynch: Peter Deming, Barry Gifford, Laura Dern, Mary Sweeney, Olga Neuwirth, Ann Kroeber, and most of all, Fred Elmes and Jack Fisk. Thanks as well to the various editors who have worked with me on Lynch-related pieces: Ann Kolson at the *New York Times*, Mark Peranson at *Cinema Scope*, John Swansburg at *Slate*, Abby McGanney Nolan and Jessica Winter at the *Village Voice*, Noah Isenberg at *Film Quarterly*, Don McMahon and Julian Rose at *Artforum*. I wrote this book while working at the Film Society of Lincoln Center, and could not have done so without the support of my comrades in the programming department, most of all Florence Almozini. I was lucky to have research assistants who were not just diligent but also insightful: Mary Elizabeth Borkowski, Ben Kenigsberg, David Gregory Lawson, Lisa Locascio, John MacDonald, and Marion Miclet. Many friends and colleagues offered suggestions and encouragement long before this book had even begun to take shape, including Melissa Anderson, Andrés Duque, Leo Goldsmith, B. Kite, Susie Linfield, Tom McCormack, and Andréa Picard. A special thanks to those who, in myriad ways, helped me see this book to its end: John Bruce, Steven Mears, Dan Sullivan, and Athina Rachel Tsangari.

Bibliography

T HIS BOOK DRAWS from Lynch's own words in *Catching the Big Fish: Meditation, Consciousness, and Creativity* (Tarcher, 2006) and Chris Rodley's indispensable book-length interview, *Lynch on Lynch* (Faber and Faber, 2005), as well as from several interviews I conducted with Lynch: in New York City in October 2001, in Los Angeles in September 2006, and over the phone in December 2007. Several of the other interviews cited can be found in *David Lynch: Interviews* (University Press of Mississippi, 2009), a career-spanning anthology edited by Richard A. Barney.

My thoughts on Lynch and his work have been shaped by a wide range of critical, academic, and journalistic writing. The following books, articles, and talks, listed in chronological order, were invaluable: J. Hoberman and Jonathan Rosenbaum's account of the making of *Eraserhead* in *Midnight Movies* (Da Capo, 1983); Michel Chion's *David Lynch* (British Film Institute, 1992); David Foster Wallace's "David Lynch Keeps His Head," first published in *Premiere* and anthologized in *A Supposedly Fun Thing I'll Never Do Again* (Little, Brown, 1997); Slavoj Žižek's *The Art of the Ridiculous Sublime: On David Lynch's Lost Highway* (University of Washington Press, 2000); the chapters on Lynch in Greil Marcus's *The Shape of Things to Come: Prophecy and the American Voice* (Picador, 2007); Greg Olson's *David Lynch: Beautiful Dark* (Scarecrow Press,

2008); Tom McCarthy's talk "The Prosthetic Imagination of David Lynch," delivered at the Tate Modern in 2010; Nicholas Rombes's "The *Blue Velvet* Project," a close reading of the film published over the course of a year (2011–2012) at filmmaker magazine.com; and Justus Nieland's *David Lynch* (University of Illinois Press, 2012).

The catalogues of the following exhibitions were extremely helpful in charting the development of Lynch's visual art career: *The Air Is on Fire* (Fondation Cartier, Paris, 2007), *Dark Splendor* (Max Ernst Museum, Brühl, Germany, 2009), and *The Unified Field* (The Pennsylvania Academy of the Fine Arts, Philadelphia, 2014).

Selected Filmography

Eraserhead, 1978
The Elephant Man, 1980
Dune, 1984
Blue Velvet, 1986
Twin Peaks, 1990–1991
Wild at Heart, 1990
Twin Peaks: Fire Walk with Me, 1992
Lost Highway, 1997
The Straight Story, 1999
Mulholland Drive, 2001
Inland Empire, 2006